Elderly Housing

Elderly Housing

A Guide to Appraisal, Market Analysis, Development, and Financing

Arthur E. Gimmy, MAI
and
Michael G. Boehm

American Institute of Real Estate Appraisers
430 North Michigan Avenue
Chicago, Illinois 60611-4088

For Educational Purposes Only

The opinions and statements set forth herein do not necessarily reflect the viewpoint of the American Institute of Real Estate Appraisers or its individual members, and neither the Institute nor its editors and staff assume responsibility for such expressions of opinion or statements.

Printed in the United States of America

Library of Congress Cataloging-in-Publication Data

Gimmy, Arthur E.
    Elderly housing : a guide to appraisal, market analysis, development, and financing / Arthur E. Gimmy and Michael G. Boehm.
        p.   cm.
    Bibliography: p.
    ISBN 0-911780-92-0 : $27.00
    1. Aged—Housing.   I. Boehm, Michael G.   II. Title.
HD7287.9.G48   1988
363.5'9—dc19   88-11999
                                                                                      CIP

Contents

Foreword

Elderly Housing: A Guide to Appraisal, Market Analysis, Development, and Financing represents a comprehensive treatment of one of the most active development industries in the United States—providing housing and related services to the elderly. In the past decade, several hundred new elderly housing facilities have been built in response to dramatic changes in our nation's demographic composition. The elderly population is growing twice as fast as the overall population, and people are living active lives at advanced ages as never before.

Despite the unquestionable surge in the healthy elderly population, some retirement housing and elderly housing projects have failed, illustrating that the mere existence of a population group does not automatically create large shifts in housing patterns. Although some developers have moved rapidly to build elderly housing, senior citizens have been slow in relinquishing the independence of their homes. The wave of seniors relocating to congregate housing facilities, predicted by some early developers and demographers, has yet to happen.

Authors Gimmy and Boehm take a thorough and logical approach to elderly housing. The organization and writing are clear whether or not the reader has had much exposure to this market. They have comprehensively divided a complex topic into logical segments and have provided a complete and lasting guide to the key elements of elderly housing evaluation which should be useful to any appraiser, developer, consultant, lender, or investor involved in this emerging industry.

The Appraisal Institute gratefully acknowledges the contributions of authors Arthur E. Gimmy, MAI, and Michael G. Boehm, as well as reviewers, Howard C. Gelbtuch, MAI, James E. Gibbons, MAI, and Thomas A. Motta, MAI, who shared with them their ideas in the preparation of this important publication.

Terrell R. Oetzel, MAI
1988 President
American Institute of Real Estate Appraisers

Acknowledgments

The authors would like to recognize the substantial contribution of Ariel Ambruster in the research, preparation, and editing of this monograph. Her aggressiveness, optimism, and talent made writing this text more enjoyable than expected. We wish her good luck and good sources in her career in journalism.

Arthur E. Gimmy, MAI

Michael G. Boehm

About the Authors

Arthur E. Gimmy, MAI, is president and owner of Arthur Gimmy International, a real estate appraisal and consulting firm based in San Francisco, California. Operating on a nationwide basis, Mr. Gimmy has had extensive experience in valuation counseling and expert testimony on numerous property types since 1955. Mr. Gimmy has a bachelor's degree in business education and master's degree in education from the University of California at Los Angeles. In addition to membership in the Appraisal Institute, he is a member and past president of Valuation Network, Inc., a nationwide consortium of leading appraisal firms throughout the United States. Mr. Gimmy has contributed to *The Appraisal Journal* and other financial publications. He is also the author of *Tennis Clubs and Racquet Sports Projects*, published by the Appraisal Institute in 1978. In recent years, he has lectured and written on key issues in the senior housing industry.

Michael G. Boehm is an appraisal associate with Arthur Gimmy International and directs their Division of Health Care and Retirement Projects. Mr. Boehm specializes in the appraisal and feasibility analysis of all types of elderly housing and has completed over 60 appraisals and studies of senior citizen housing projects throughout the country. Mr. Boehm has a bachelor's degree in accounting from Northern Illinois University and a master's degree in business administration from Northwestern University. Mr. Boehm has been working toward his designation from the Appraisal Institute since 1985.

Introduction

For many years, "elderly housing" meant a nursing facility, a board-and-care home, or a Florida resort village. Today, a definition for the term is becoming much harder to pin down. The elderly housing market is undergoing a dramatic evolution, characterized by new housing forms, a wide variety of services, and rapid growth. Developers all over the country are being drawn to the elderly housing industry, expanding the concept as they design projects that address previously unmet needs. Once the domain of nonprofit groups, elderly housing now sparks interest in private developers and financial institutions. Some predict it will soon be as big an industry as housing for singles has been in the past.

What is attracting developers has been described as one of the biggest demographic discoveries of the century: the number of elderly in the United States is growing rapidly, at a rate twice as fast as that of the overall population. This means a solidly growing market for elderly housing through the year 2025. The number of people 65 and over is expected to double by that time, and in the same period it is projected that the number of those over 85 will quadruple. By the year 2000, people aged 55 and over will make up 22% of the U.S. population. This new surge of retirees is breaking the stereotype of the elderly as poor, frail, and dependent. Today's elderly remain active longer, strive for independence, and are often quite capable of paying for the living options they desire.

This new wave of housing development aims to provide residential and service options where, in the past, none have existed. Until recently, the lack of choices in the housing market forced the elderly to choose between the expense of resort retirement centers or the isolation of nursing homes. But many retirees, while no longer young and vigorous, are not yet ready for an "old folks' home." They want to remain as independent as possible, even though they may occasionally need a hand with housework, transportation, cooking, or personal care.

To meet these demands, new forms of elderly housing incorporate services previously associated only with hotels, hospitals, or community senior centers. Facilities often offer meals, social activities, transportation, and linen and housekeeping services. They may make available personal, intermediate, or skilled nursing care, if needed, or contract with a nearby hospital to provide medical or emergency care.

As the capabilities of the elderly vary, so do the shelters and care systems offered them, resulting in the tremendous variety in the number and combination of services offered today. Facilities range from the minimum of providing shelter, as in noncongregate senior apartments and single-family dwellings, to the maximum of care and service offered in intermediate and skilled nursing facilities. This emerging spectrum in elderly housing, stretching from independence to dependence, contrasts sharply with the large gap in options available to seniors in the past. A graphic depiction of this spectrum, with its numerous options and amenities, is shown in Table 1.1.

Table 1.1. A Continuum of Elderly Housing

Elderly Housing Type	Empty-nester Homes	Retirement Apartments	Retirement Communities	Congregate—Low-end	Congregate—High-end	CCRC/Lifecare	Residential Care Facility	Skilled Nursing Facility	Hospital
AGE	45-85	55-85	55-85	65-85	70-85	70-85	75+	80+	65+
Single-unit independent housing	■	□	▨	□	□	▨	□	□	□
Multi-unit housing	□	■	▨	■	■	▨	■	■	■
Kitchens in units	■	■	■	■	■	▨	□	□	□
Equity ownership	■	▨	■	□	□	▨	□	□	□
Grounds upkeep	□	■	■	■	■	■	■	■	■
Extensive outdoor recreation	□	□	■	▨	▨	▨	▨	▨	▨
Security	□	□	▨	■	■	■	■	■	■
Specialized management	□	□	▨	■	■	■	■	■	■
Indoor recreation/activities	□	□	▨	▨	■	■	■	■	□
Transportation	□	□	▨	▨	■	■	■	■	□
Emergency call buttons	□	□	□	▨	■	■	■	■	■
Housekeeping, linens	□	□	□	▨	■	■	■	■	■
Common dining room/meals served	□	□	□	▨	■	■	■	■	■
Fee for service	□	□	□	□	▨	■	▨	■	■
Licensed	□	□	□	□	□	▨	■	■	■
Personal care	□	□	□	□	□	▨	▨	■	■
Intermediate or skilled care	□	□	□	□	□	▨	□	■	■
Acute medical care	□	□	□	□	□	□	□	□	■

Key:
■ Generally Available   ▨ Sometimes Available   □ Generally Not Available

SOURCE: Arthur Gimmy International

2

Complexity of Elderly Market

The market for these new forms of elderly housing is believed to be extensive. One industry expert predicts a need for more than 812,000 new units in retirement centers and 116,000 new units in lifecare centers by the year 2000.[1] But though the need is clear and the long-term demographics favorable, analyzing the elderly market is complex. Industry experts stress that developing a successful facility requires more than just constructing shelter. It requires lengthy planning and sensitivity to the special design needs of the elderly, such as extra security, proper lighting, and conveniently placed fixtures. It requires experienced management of meals, maintenance, and social services. Clearly, developing elderly housing involves more than bricks and mortar.

The national senior market, though broad, is shallow. Many developers are aggressively entering this newly discovered arena, and competition has grown fierce in many regions. Some lenders are already warning that certain areas are reaching the point of overbuilding.

Beyond developer eagerness is the problem of caution on the part of seniors. Market experts are unsure of the extent of demand for the newer facilities because the limits of market penetration for such developments have yet to be tested. Many seniors living in their own homes are unfamiliar with what the elderly housing market is offering. Consequently, developers need to devote extra funds to marketing and education. Also, the elderly sector, being composed of a large percentage of experienced home-buyers, can be highly discriminating. Lifecare communities, the most complex and expensive elderly housing alternative, report an extended lease-up period, averaging about 18 months but sometimes stretching as long as three years. Buyers often make six to ten visits to a facility before reaching a decision. In addition, the overwhelming majority of seniors continue to live in their own homes and show less propensity for moving than the general population. Often, it is a tragedy, such as the death of a spouse or a debilitating illness, that compels them to look for new quarters. When they do move, they often prefer to remain within the same community.

Market Subgroups Among the Elderly

The days are gone when the elderly sector could be viewed as monolithic. Instead, demand for housing varies among regions, and among varying groups within the elderly market. The mature market is commonly divided into two major segments. The first is the pre-retirement or "empty nester" group, whose members range in age from 50 to 64 years. Although many in this age group are still employed, these pre-retirees often encounter a shift in lifestyle that prompts a desire for a different form of housing. Empty nesters tend to prefer scaled-down, single-family homes, condominiums, or townhouses that require less maintenance and eliminate the extra space once required for children.

---

[1] John D. Valiante, "The Capital Requirements for Long-Term Care Services," *Healthcare Financial Management*, April 1984, p. 84.

The second segment consists those seniors over 65. Market observers divide this group into three submarkets: the "young-old" or "go-go" seniors, aged 65 to 74; the elderly or "slow-go" group, aged 75 to 85; and the "old-old" or "no-go" seniors, aged 85 and over. The size and growth trends for the three submarkets are shown in Figure 1.1.

Figure 1.1. Numbers of Elderly per Subgroup

Three Markets
(numbers of elderly in millions, 1986 estimates)

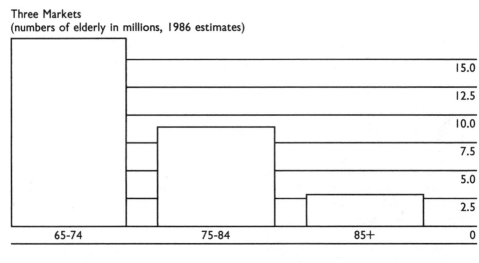

Market Growth
(growth of elderly in millions)

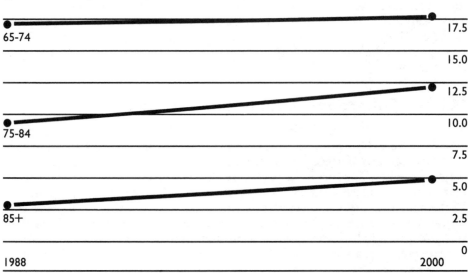

SOURCE: U.S. Bureau of the Census, *Projections of the Population of the United States by Age, Sex and Race, 1983 to 2080*, Current Populations Reports, Series P-25, No. 952 (1984).

Young retirees are active, independent, and interested in enjoying their leisure to the fullest. Resort retirement housing, with its sunny environment, wide range of outdoor activities, and spacious luxury dwellings, is geared toward this group. The emphasis is on recreation rather than care.

Seniors in the middle group are beginning to come to terms with their physical limitations. They are slowing down and require more care than young retirees, but at the same time are trying to preserve their independence and privacy. They represent the most significant discovery in the elderly market— the group that is most stymied by the lack, until recently, of specially tailored elderly housing options. Congregate and lifecare facilities, emphasizing as much independence as possible with a minimal amount of care, have cropped up as alternatives for this submarket. These facilities provide services to take care of the cooking and the housecleaning, and may have personal or medical care waiting on call, should the need arise.

Many members of the oldest elderly, though often frail and requiring care, are not sick and can be expected to live a long life. Lifecare projects also meet the needs of the old-old group and remove the necessity of their residents moving as abilities and limitations change. Residential care and intermediate and skilled nursing facilities are designed for persons with medical difficulties.

The newest types of facilities, the congregate centers and continuing care facilities, arose to fill a gap in the market and address a social need prevalent among the elderly. Getting old means facing unpleasant reality: The body doesn't work as well as it used to, and one's parameters are shrinking. While perhaps needing help with everyday chores, dressing, or bathing, seniors still yearn for their full independence. The long-established retirement resort towns and nursing homes often fail to address this dichotomy. However, many new, multifaceted projects are reaching this unmet need by offering a wide range and different levels of care.

The new congregate facility, known also as the adult congregate living facility (ACLF), not only provides housing; it is similar to a hotel, with meal preparation, housekeeping, and linen service. It also serves a social function, often providing transportation to events or shopping areas and space such as craft rooms, film centers, and libraries for indoor activities and social events.

The new continuing-care retirement center (CCRC) provides a form of insurance through health care to ease the fears of seniors that future infirmities might lead to money problems or relocation. CCRCs, like lifecare facilities in existence for a number of years, provide a range of different environments. The new resident lives in an independent unit, knowing that, should she or he need it, a personal care service or facility is available, as well as an infirmary or skilled nursing unit.

This book will examine the broad range of shelter options available to seniors today. The specific focus, however, will remain on the congregate and continuum-of-care facilities, those new forms of housing that have appeared on the scene in response to the burgeoning numbers of seniors. The book will aim to serve as an introduction for the builder, developer, manager, lender, investor, appraiser, and consultant to the basic trends and characteristics of the retirement housing field, and will provide guidelines for both determining the feasibility of a project and providing valuation estimates for congregate and continuing-care housing.

Following this introduction, Chapter Two provides an examination of the demographic shift that is fueling developer interest in retirement housing. Chapter Three presents an overview of the many types of senior housing options now available. Chapter Four examines at a macro level what makes retirement housing unique: the varied market preferences, peculiarities of design that make senior living easier, and locational considerations, all vital determinants of the feasibility of a senior development.

Another characteristic that can spell success or failure for a retirement project is its management—how food service, social activities, upkeep, and health care are juggled in order to create an inviting and supportive lifestyle for senior residents. This is discussed in Chapter Five.

With the well-publicized bankruptcy of West Coast-based Pacific Homes in the 1970s, methods of financing continuing care facilities and other forms of senior housing took center stage. Chapter Six first discusses options for financing both profit and non-profit retirement centers, and then examines the pros and cons of each financing method. This chapter presents and analyzes the results of a comprehensive questionnaire sent to major lenders of senior housing in the United States.

From there, the focus narrows to micro-level demand in Chapter Seven and on how the market saturation of competing facilities, regional characteristics and a focused bundle of services combine to determine an individual project's feasibility.

Chapters Eight and Nine present various approaches to estimating the value of different types of senior housing projects from an appraiser's perspective. This includes value determination using a cost, market comparison and income approach. Our analysis emphasizes the unique considerations imperative in the effective valuation of senior housing.

Finally, the book concludes with detailed case studies including project and valuation statistics. The studies present operating revenue and expense data on several types of facilities giving a general picture of variations in the industry.

2

History and Demographics

Development and Growth of the Elderly Housing Market

Although it has only been in recent years that both the number and variety of retirement facilities have expanded, the idea of a home tailored to the needs of the elderly has a long history. A brief chronology of important events in elderly housing in this country can be found in Table 2.1. There are reports of continuing care facilities in existence as early as the American Revolution. Throughout the nineteenth century, homes for the aged were commonly established by religious and fraternal organizations, a practice arising from shelters designed for retired ministers and missionaries. The number of these retirement homes grew after 1940 concurrent with a nationwide religious revival and increased church membership.

During the same era, in the depths of the Depression in 1935, the U.S. Government passed the Social Security Act into law, establishing the idea that an entity other than the family could be responsible for the economic security of older citizens. These two developments helped lay the groundwork for the greater affluence enjoyed by today's elderly. Adding to this current affluence was the creation in 1940 of the G. I. Bill's low-cost housing loan program, which enabled veterans to purchase the homes that have become the cornerstone of the economic security of many elderly individuals today.

In 1954, a planned retirement resort project developed in Arizona by Elmer Johns and Ben Schleider launched the first wave of housing designed specifically for the affluent elderly. With the planned retirement town came the idea of active recreation and leisure in old age. As the popularity of the retirement resorts grew throughout the 1960s, lifecare communities, though a much smaller phenomenon, continued to proliferate, financed largely by tax-exempt bonds.

Table 2.1. Elderly Housing in the United States: A Short History

1880s	Chancellor Otto von Bismarck of Prussia decreed (as a political ploy) that all persons reaching age 65 would get a life pension. Life expectancy at the time was 47 years. This act determined the "proper" retirement age up to the present time.	1960	First sizeable retirement community, inspired by 1954 effort, built by Del Webb in Sun City, Arizona.
Late 1800s	First retirement housing project in U.S. Sponsored by a religious organization to provide for retired clergy.	1970	First federal congregate housing law passed. No funds for purchase or preparation of meals. Did little to stimulate production of congregate housing.
1900	Life expectancy at birth: 47 years.	1974	National Housing Act of 1959 revised to allow 40-year loans to nonprofit sponsors to build or renovate elderly housing.
1900-1930	Heavy immigration of young adults contributed to size of elderly population from 1965 to present.		
1935	Social Security enacted. Provided for retirement benefits at age 65.	1975	Permanent financing source for HUD 202 program provided.
1937	Housing Act of 1937. First federal involvement in housing for the elderly.	1978	Housing Services Act of 1978. Gave impetus to congregate housing by providing money for meals and some services. Thirty-eight congregate developments were built in next 36 months.
1940s	G. I. Bill increases education level of young adults. Low-cost housing loans encourage children to establish separate homes, most often in suburbs. Marks start of the loss of family togetherness. Laid foundation for today's elderly housing market.	1979	About 100 lifecare projects in operation.
		Late 1970s	More retirement housing built. Elderly's housing options increased. Some landmark financial failures occurred.
1950	Retirement housing market starts as World War I generation begins to reach retirement age. Choices of good retirement facilities in customer's hometown quite limited. Out-of-area retirement communities do well.	1980	Subsidized housing programs start to decline as percentage of total housing built. Uniform Barrier-Free Design Act drafted and made available to all states.
			American National Standards Institute revises Elderly Housing Design Standards (ANSI 117.1). HUD issues revised design criteria.
1954	First planned active retirement community built in Arizona by Elmer Johns and Ben Schleifer.	1984-Present	Lower construction costs stimulate production of elderly housing.
1956	FHA 207; FHA allowed to insure mortgages on elderly housing.	1985	One person in ten is 65+ years old; 65+ population growing at 5,000 per day.
1958	First public housing project completed built specifically for the elderly.	1986	325 to 700 lifecare projects in operation. Approximately 865 congregate housing projects. Over 20,000 nursing homes in operation. Life expectancy at birth: 74 years.
1959	HUD 202; National Housing Act of 1959 enacted. Direct loans to nonprofit sponsors authorized.		

SOURCE: Grubb & Ellis, *Investor Outlook* (Second Quarter 1986). Reprinted with permission.

Problems in lifecare communities began to surface in the mid-seventies, however, when a number of facilities defaulted on debts or declared bankruptcy. Prominent among these failures was Pacific Homes, a West Coast-based, nonprofit group associated with the Methodist Church that ran seven communities and went bankrupt in 1977. In another incident, a minister in Alabama was jailed in 1981 for securities fraud after defaulting on $2.1 million in bonds for a lifecare community. Financial troubles such as these led the Federal Trade Commission to begin investigating the industry's management and marketing practices in 1978. Though the commission never found violations of trade laws, it did enter into a consent agreement with a company that managed 50 lifecare projects in numerous states to cease and desist from certain "unfair and deceptive" practices. The investigation, however, resulted in no concrete regulatory action by the federal government. At present, regulation remains a state responsibility. Thirteen states have passed regulations covering lifecare facilities, and one—New York—prohibits facilities from offering lifecare contracts. Florida and California require projects to presell 50% of units before receiving financing. Increased regulation will tend to raise development and operating costs for health-related facilities.

Despite the increased scrutiny, regulation has not caused the construction of these projects to abate. For-profit corporations have taken over an industry previously dominated by nonprofit, often church-related organizations. These new companies have altered facility fee structures, begun to analyze actuarial assumptions, and provided the kinds of amenities necessary to create and nurture a unique target market. This increased sophistication has become more critical to establishing a financially secure base for the profitable development and operation of an elderly housing project. Today, for example, most continuum-of-care facilities are labeled "continuing-care retirement centers" or CCRCs, and offer services on a fee-for-service basis or through an adjustable monthly fee, rather than through a single endowment payment that often assured care for life in the past. Lately, major lodging and health care firms, such as the Marriott Corporation, have entered the market. At the same time, proprietary and nonprofit groups have formed partnerships to take advantage of tax laws and government funding. Major operators and developers in the retirement housing industry are shown in Table 2.2.

Table 2.2. Major Operators and Developers in the Retirement Housing Industry

Top Ten For-Profit Operators			
Name	Facilities/Units	Name	Facilities/Units
1. Life Care Services	30/8,453	6. Basic American Retirement	7/1,583
2. Retirement Centers of America	17/4,232	7. Ebenezer Society	10/1,519
3. Southmark Retirement Communities	26/3,588	8. Forum Group	12/1,457
4. General Health Management	14/2,659	9. Cambridge Group	5/1,157
5. Beverly Enterprises	17/2,459	10. Leisure Care	10/842

Table 2.2. Major Operators and Developers in the Retirement Housing Industry— continued

Top Ten Nonprofit Operators

Name	Facilities/Units	Name	Facilities/Units
1. National Benevolent Society	50/6,581	6. Lutheran Social Services—Illinois	16/1,754
2. National Church Residences	89/6,206	7. North California Presbyterian Homes	6/1,498
3. Adult Communities Total Services	12/3,141	8. South California Presbyterian Homes	11/1,454
4. American Baptist Homes— West	13/2,895	9. Lutheran Social Services—Michigan	8/1,061
5. Covenant Retirement Communities	12/1,827	10. Presbyterian Manors of Mid-America	15/1,000

Ten Most Active Developers

Name	Facilities/Units	Name	Facilities/Units
1. RadiceCare Inc.	5/1,104	6. Charter Communities	3/750
2. Heritage Centers of America	8/1,102	7. National Housing Partnership	2/632
3. Congregate Living Systems	4/1,000	8. Forum Group	4/609
4. General Health Management	5/993	9. Retirement Centers of America	2/503
5. Presbyterian Homes of New Jersey	3/900	10. Basic American Retirement	4/446

SOURCE: Steve Rogers, "Survey Reveals Continued Growth for Retirement Housing Industry." *Contemporary Long Term Care* (June 1987): p. 45.

In summary, recent years have witnessed the following industry trends.

- Emergence of proprietary, chain-sponsored developers and operators
- Joint venturing of larger corporations and small developers
- Variety of contract options, with primary focus on high-quality, luxury rental projects
- Interest of hospital and skilled nursing chain operators in industry
- Greater emphasis on product design and competitive fee structures
- Partially refundable entry fees at CCRC projects
- Breaking up services and amenities into a fee-for-service structure
- Greater market targeting and segmentation of product type
- Growing, though still limited, lender acceptance of elderly housing proposals
- Use of cooperative and condominium forms
- Segregation of on-site health-related service and hospitalized residents from congregate living residents
- Realization that marketing is a key determinant of project absorption success

- Increased use of primary market research to forecast demand
- Larger unit sizes
- Optional financing programs at a single facility, such as buy-ins and rentals
- Increasing government regulation

Growth in Number of Elderly

For many years, the predominance of the baby boom generation in the public's mind has overshadowed other generations, notably the wave of young immigrants who came to the United States in the early years of the twentieth century. This large population, now elderly, has remained significant through the advancements in technology and medicine that have increased life expectancy by 26 years since 1900. In 1984, people aged 65 could expect to enjoy, on average, 16.8 additional years in their lifetimes. The result is a generation of elderly persons that has grown at twice the rate of the population at large.

Today the elderly make up one-eighth of the population, or about 30 million people. This is an increase of 130% from 1950, when about 12 million seniors lived in this country. It is estimated that by the year 2000, the elderly will make up more than one-fifth of the population, or about 65 million people.

Growth in Buying Power

Developers are attracted not only by the number of elderly persons, but also by their wealth. Gradually, people are beginning to realize that the elderly are not as poor as they may have been in the past. Today's elderly are the first generation of seniors that has accumulated a substantial financial base. The average senior citizen has two to three times the discretionary buying power of younger home buyers. Put another way, one-half of all discretionary income—estimated at $97 billion—is controlled by people aged 50 and over.

This trend is likely to continue, as evidenced by the explosive growth in the 1980s of individual retirement accounts or IRAs. Employed Americans may also be more inclined these days to set aside funds for their own retirement as a way of hedging against the possibly shaky future of the Social Security system. Today's elderly have benefited from private pensions, investment of assets, and increases in Social Security payments since 1960. Because of these safety nets, the poverty rate among the elderly dropped from 28% in 1966 to 14% in 1984, while the rate for Americans aged 18 to 64 hovered between 9% and 12%.

Although many think that the "fixed income" status of seniors leaves them vulnerable, it has actually protected them, via automatic Social Security cost-of-living increases, from the inflation spirals of the 1970s and cushioned them against the income loss suffered by younger Americans as a whole in the late 1970s and early 1980s. In fact, because of these fixed-income protections, in 1985 the poverty rate of the elderly fell below that of the general population for the first time.

Table 2.3. Actual and Projected Growth of the Older Population, 1900-2050
(Numbers in thousands)

Year	Total pop. all ages	55 to 64 Years		65 to 74 Years		75 to 84 Years		85 Years and Over		65 Years and Over	
		No.	%	No.	%	No.	%	No.	%	No.	%
1900	76,303	4,009	5.3	2,189	2.9	772	1.0	123	0.2	3,084	4.0
1910	91,972	5,054	5.5	2,793	3.0	989	1.1	167	0.2	3,950	4.3
1920	105,711	6,532	6.2	3,464	3.3	1,259	1.2	210	0.2	4,933	4.7
1930	122,775	8,397	6.8	4,721	3.8	1,641	1.3	272	0.2	6,634	5.4
1940	131,669	10,572	8.0	6,375	4.8	2,278	1.7	365	0.3	9,019	6.8
1950	150,967	13,295	8.8	8,415	5.6	3,278	2.2	577	0.4	12,270	8.1
1960	179,323	15,572	8.7	10,997	6.1	4,633	2.6	929	0.5	16,560	9.2
1970	203,302	18,608	9.2	12,447	6.1	6,124	3.0	1,409	0.7	19,980	9.8
1980	226,505	21,700	9.6	15,578	6.9	7,727	3.4	2,240	1.0	25,544	11.3
1990	249,657	21,051	8.4	18,035	7.2	10,349	4.1	3,313	1.3	31,697	12.7
2000	267,955	23,767	8.9	17,677	6.6	12,318	4.6	4,926	1.8	34,921	13.0
2010	283,238	34,848	12.3	20,318	7.2	12,326	4.4	6,551	2.3	39,195	13.8
2020	296,597	40,298	13.6	29,855	10.1	14,486	4.9	7,081	2.4	51,422	17.3
2030	304,807	34,025	11.2	34,535	11.3	21,434	7.0	8,612	2.8	64,581	21.2
2040	308,559	34,717	11.3	29,272	9.5	24,882	8.1	12,834	4.2	66,988	21.7
2050	309,488	37,327	12.1	30,114	9.7	21,263	6.9	16,034	5.2	67,411	21.8

SOURCES: U.S. Bureau of the Census, *Decennial Censuses of Population, 1990-2050*; U.S. Bureau of the Census, *Projections of the Population of the United States by Age, Sex and Race*, Current Population Reports, Series P-25, No. 952 (1984). Projections are middle series.

Figure 2.1. Income Sources, Aged Units 65 and Older, 1982

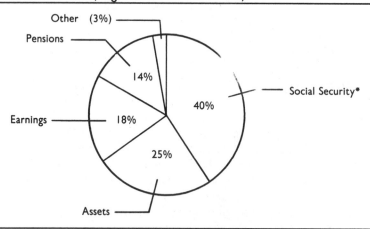

*Includes Social Security and Railroad Retirement. Railroad retirement accounts for about 1% of income for aged units.

SOURCE: Susan Grad, *Income of the Population 55 and Over* (Washington, D.C.: Social Security Administration, 1982).

Figure 2.2. Poverty Rates for Nonaged and Aged, 1966-1984

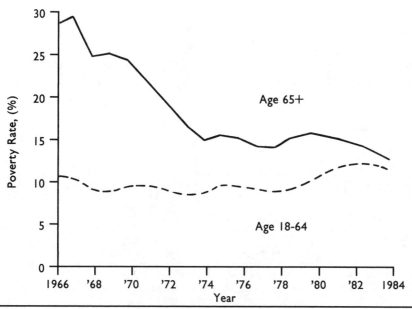

SOURCE: U.S. Bureau of the Census, *Current Population Surveys, 1967-85.*

It is not income alone, however, that has placed the elderly in such a beneficial position. Seniors earn much less in money income ($18,236 in median income in 1984) than those under 65 ($29,292). But seniors make up for this by holding substantially more assets than the nonelderly. In 1982, for example, 25% of the incomes of elderly households came from assets. This income was not distributed evenly, however: about one-third of the households reported no asset income, and only 28% received more than $5,000 per year from assets.

The resulting picture is of a widely varying age group consisting of both rich and poor. The elderly housing industry, composed of for-profit as well as government-funded housing, has at least the potential for accommodating both groups. To date, most developers have targeted their new projects to the affluent elderly.

While only 12% to 14% of the elderly live below the poverty level, a larger percentage live close to poverty than occurs among the population at large. About 37% of the elderly remain within 200% of poverty, while only about 28% of nonelderly are at that level. Nevertheless, a substantial number of seniors are able to look to the roof over their heads for financial security. The image of the hamstrung elderly couple on a fixed income has dissolved to one of an economically secure couple, sitting on top of a goldmine: their family home. Seventy-four percent of America's elderly own their own home, and 80% own it free and clear. It is estimated that older Americans have more than $600 billion locked up in home equity.

Figure 2.3. Income Distribution of Households 70 and Over

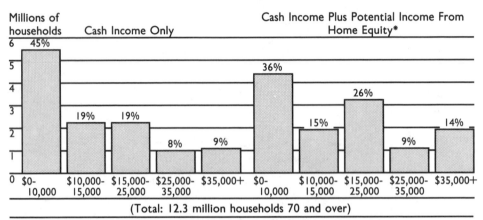

(Total: 12.3 million households 70 and over)

*Assuming homes were sold and net proceeds of sale invested at 10% per year.
SOURCE: Real Estate Research Corporation, *Rental Retirement Housing: New Opportunities* (Chicago, 1986). Analysis is based on figures from the U.S. Bureau of the Census.

Developers are counting on the income from the sale of those homes to finance entry fees and rent at continuing-care and congregate facilities. Elderly homeowners have benefited from the inflation spirals of the 1970s, which led to a 58% real increase in the average home equity of new retirees from 1969 to 1982. In 1985, the average equity in homes owned by seniors was estimated at $60,900, while a 1984 study showed that the median entry fee for one person at a continuing-care retirement center was $32,500.[1]

A Close-to-Home Group

One problem faced by developers is that many healthy seniors show a strong propensity for remaining in their own homes. These homeowners may provide only a limited market for congregate housing facilities. For example, while 23% of the U.S. population moved in 1980, only 9% of seniors aged 65 to 74 and 5% of those 70 to 84 moved. The desire among the elderly to remain near their homes limits the ability of a facility to draw from outside its immediate area.

It is possible that many seniors remain in their houses because they do not perceive any better options, but there are other benefits to staying at home.

[1] Howard E. Winklevoss and Alwyn V. Powell, *Continuing Care Retirement Communities: An Empirical, Financial and Legal Analysis* (Homewood, IL: Richard D. Irwin, 1984).

Houses that have been owned for a long time are generally "good bargains": they have appreciated in value, so an elderly owner will often get more housing per unit of cost than would be possible in a newly constructed home. In addition, there is sometimes a stigma attached to elderly housing. Study after study has shown that many seniors—even up to age 75 and beyond—feel they are not yet ready for the elderly housing alternative.

The cost of maintenance and energy is often the element that pushes an elderly homeowner to search for other housing options. Almost one-half of homes owned by seniors were built before 1940; many may need extensive repairs or renovations that are not affordable or practical for the elderly homeowner. Once the children have grown up and moved away, the upkeep of a large and largely empty house may become too difficult or less meaningful. Other reasons for desiring to move often given by seniors are the death of a spouse, decline of the neighborhood, or desire to be near family and friends. All of these reasons speak to a need for social interaction. Still, in a 1982-83 teacher pension fund survey by TIAA-CREF, a group generally more educated than the population at large, 83% expressed a preference for remaining in their own homes.

Just as most seniors seem to prefer staying in the same house, so do most seem to prefer the same town or geographic area. Developers of retirement facilities find that an overwhelming percentage of their residents are drawn from the immediate area of the facility, as much as 80% from within a 10-mile radius. Even when they do move, five-sixths of the elderly stay within 200 miles of their homes. Only a small percentage of seniors (4% in 1979) move out of state, though the number has increased by 50% from the 1960s to the 1970s.

Because seniors stay near home, the market for senior housing is not limited to the Sunbelt states. The nation's elderly households are almost evenly divided across the country: the Northeast and North-Central states each hold one-fourth of the population, one-fifth are in the West, and one-third are located in the South.

When the elderly move out of state, they are most likely to move to Florida. The northern tier states from Michigan to New York have the heaviest emigration of elderly. There is, however, a return stream. Three out of ten seniors who move to Florida return to their home state before they die. These people are part of a newly-noted trend called "countermigration." They are more likely to be frail, poor, and living in institutions, and often return home to be near relatives in their last years.

Living Longer

At the turn of the century, the average person could expect to live to be 47 years old. Today, 25 years have been added to that figure, so that the average person has a life expectancy of 72. Moreover, persons reaching the age of 65 can expect to live an additional 16.8 years.

Figure 2.4. Percentage of Population 65 Years and Older, Counties with 15% or More, 1980

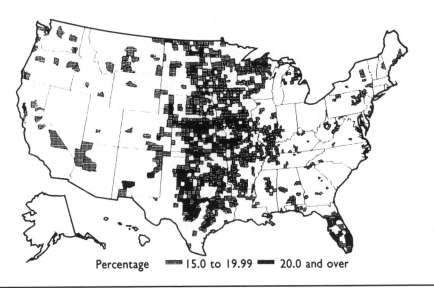

Percentage   ▦ 15.0 to 19.99   ■ 20.0 and over

SOURCE: U.S. Bureau of the Census, *Decennial Census of the Population, 1980*. Prepared by Michael Callahan, U.S. Senate Computer Center.

Figure 2.5. Life Expectancy at Birth, 1940-1982

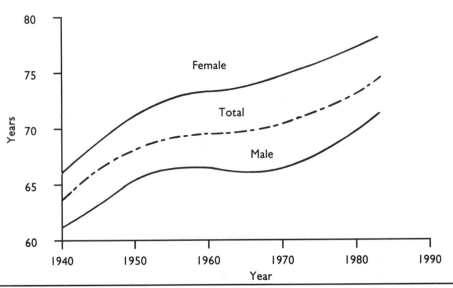

SOURCE: National Center for Health Statistics, *Monthly Vital Statistics Report*, Vol. 33, No. 9 (1984).

Table 2.4. Life Expectancy at Birth and Age 65 by Sex and Calendar Year, 1900-2050

Year	Male		Female	
	At Birth	At Age 65	At Birth	At Age 65
1900	46.4	11.3	49.0	12.0
1910	50.1	11.4	53.6	12.1
1920	54.5	11.8	56.3	12.3
1930	58.0	11.8	61.3	12.9
1940	61.4	11.9	65.7	13.4
1950	65.6	12.8	71.1	15.1
1960	66.7	12.9	73.2	15.9
1970	67.1	13.1	74.9	17.1
1980	69.9	14.0	77.5	18.4
1990	71.4	14.5	78.9	19.2
2000	72.1	14.8	79.5	19.5
2010	72.4	15.0	79.8	19.8
2020	72.7	15.2	80.1	20.1
2030	73.0	15.4	80.4	20.3
2040	73.3	15.6	80.7	20.6
2050	73.6	15.8	81.0	20.8

SOURCE: Social Security Administration, *Social Security Area Population Projections.* Actuarial Study No. 92, Alternative I (1984).

While they are living longer, seniors are not necessarily living in a state of perfect health. The elderly, who make up only 12% of the population, account for a disproportionate amount—about one-third—of total health care expenditures. In 1982, 20% of those over 65 were hospitalized at some point, compared with 9% of those younger than 65. Yet the elderly as a group are healthier today than in the past. Medical advances, emphasis on nonsmoking, exercise, and proper diet have led to a better quality of life physically.

Although they are healthier, seniors are finding that their medical bills are no less expensive when they become ill. Expenditures for elderly health care increased significantly in recent years, forcing hospitals, the federal government, and the elderly themselves to search for solutions. At present, the average annual health care payments for the elderly, excluding premium payments, range from $1,000 to $1,700. To lower costs in the face of government limitations on Medicare payments, hospitals are considering releasing patients earlier into less intense and less costly health care facilities. This process could go further: some experts have estimated that up to 40% of nursing home patients do not need to be there. The newer housing facilities, which combine personal care or skilled care options with independent living options, could address this need.

Women Make Up Large Part of Population

Proprietors of senior housing are finding that their residential population is largely made up of women. In fact, the senior population has become more female through time. In 1960, elderly women outnumbered elderly men five to four; today that figure is three to two.

Significantly different social patterns exist for the two sexes over 65, and these differences increase as age increases. In 1984, most elderly men over 75 (70%) were married, but most women that age (67%) were widowed. This disparity is caused not only by varying death rates between the sexes, but also by the tendency among men to marry younger women.

A Caveat

Although it is clear that the number of the elderly, their good health, and their wealth have all increased, it is less clear how much of an impact these increases will have on the housing market in the short run. The industry cannot depend on continuous growth in the number of all age groups within the 65-and-over market. The recent expansion of the number of seniors consists of those born before the Depression. But because fewer children were born during the Depression and World War II, the number of "young old" is expected to remain steady and will not increase substantially until 2010, when the baby boom generation reaches retirement age.

Until that time, the greatest increase in the elderly by far will be among the very old—those aged 85 and over, most of whom are women living alone. By 1995, this segment is projected to jump by more than 50% to over 4 million. This age group has less money and requires more services and health care than first-generation retirees. They are part of a new phenomenon, the growth of the "frail elderly." In what one observer has called the "survival of the unfittest," more and more people are remaining alive longer, but often living in a state of frailty, helplessness, or disability. Forty-six percent of those 85 and over need functional assistance, defined as a need for the assistance of another person to perform one or more personal-care or home-management activities.

This group will need the extended services and care provided by continuing-care facilities, and, to a lesser extent, congregate centers. Many will need to enter intermediate or skilled nursing facilities. At the same time, skilled nursing facilities could lose residents to the new forms of elderly housing. Studies suggest that a large number of residents of skilled nursing facilities—estimates range from 15% to 40%—do not really need nursing home care. The more limited health services offered at residential care and lifecare facilities could allow these seniors to live somewhat more independently.

3

Types of Retirement Projects

The elderly are an extremely heterogeneous group, and no one form of elderly housing can appeal to them all. Choosing housing is often a weighty decision for a senior, who will look for a facility specifically tailored to his or her needs and lifestyle. Today, that search for a perfect fit in housing may be easier. Developers are expanding beyond standard homes and apartments to facilities that provide barrier-free access, health services, extensive recreation opportunities, and enticing locations. They are building housing to suit many different capabilities and income levels.

The range of elderly housing options begins with the mere provision of shelter for those who are totally independent, and ends with a skilled nursing facility where housing has been transformed into a total life-support system for the frailest of seniors. Today, the most sophisticated facilities offer a multi-layered package of services. Aside from basic shelter, the various services offered can generally be divided into those usually associated with hotels, those associated with social work, and those associated with hospitals.

Hotel-oriented services take care of routine tasks and normal upkeep. They include housekeeping, linen cleaning and changing, meals, forms of security, and grounds maintenance.

Social work services keep the elderly active and interacting with other people and with the world around them. These services include transportation to shopping centers and cultural events, counseling, and planning of activities, clubs, and programs.

Lastly, hospital services include health counseling, contracts with outside health facilities, exercise programs, referral services, nutrition programs, health checkups by visiting medical personnel, a staff nurse, or in-house health care through an infirmary, personal care facility, intermediate facility, or skilled nursing facility.

Retirement Communities

New retirees or those not quite yet retired often seek an active life in an untroubled environment. These young seniors, typically 50 to 70 years old, often married, and ready to enjoy their new freedom, are the target market for retirement communities.

About one million seniors live in an estimated 2,400 large-scale retirement communities across the United States, though most are clustered in the Sunbelt region. These communities are self-contained towns emphasizing a luxurious and leisurely retirement lifestyle, combined with activities at numerous recreational amenities such as golf courses, swimming pools, and tennis courts. Retirement villages and subdivisions can also be included in this category. These projects, again, are marketed for healthy, active, usually married retirees, but they are smaller in scope and size than retirement communities and usually depend on cultural, financial, and health facilities in the surrounding urban area.

At the top end of the scale are extensive retirement towns with populations of up to 50,000 people, such as Sun City, Arizona, with 47,500 residents, or Leisure World in Orange County, California, with a population of 25,000. These enormous projects pioneered the concept of the retirement community during the 1950s and 1960s, when, for the first time, the idea of a leisurely, independent, and financially secure old age became widespread. Today, the trend in retirement communities is toward the smaller development with fewer expensive recreational facilities.

These large communities, generally created by large development corporations, offer a wide range of housing options, from single-family homes to townhouses and condominiums. The towns have their own shopping centers, restaurants, financial institutions, local newspapers, and health facilities, often including a complete hospital. Residents typically have access to numerous types of recreational facilities, as well; Sun City, for example, has 11 golf courses, seven swimming pools, 72 shuffleboard courts, 17 tennis courts, and eight lawn bowling greens.

These types of communities may have restricted access or may contain special security features. The only restriction usually placed on residents is that they be at least 50 years old. Seniors choosing a retirement community tend to be in the middle or upper-middle income bracket.

The smaller villages and subdivisions can range in number of residents from 500 to 5,000. The type of housing and the number and kind of services offered varies widely. Some are groupings of single-family detached homes, while others are a cluster of four-plexes or apartment buildings. Mobile home parks fall into this category as well. Tenure arrangements range from full ownership to cooperatives, condominiums, or rentals. Residents are often tied together through a set of services, such as a security arrangement or use of a swimming pool and clubhouse, for which they pay a set monthly fee. Subdivisions may provide the elderly with little more than an age limitation, ensuring a certain type of social homogeneity. These would function as a suburban neighborhood with a predominance of elderly residents interacting freely with the community outside the facility. Other villages or subdivisions are self-contained worlds, providing commercial and cultural facilities to residents.

Retirement Apartments

An option for the less wealthy, but still healthy, retiree is the retirement apartment. Aside from an age restriction for residents, retirement apartments are essentially the same as standard apartments except for certain design features such as raised electrical outlets and more accessible kitchen cabinets. Though these developments are noncongregate in that they do not offer common dining areas and other amenities, they can meet an elderly resident's social needs. Government-assisted programs, such as Meals on Wheels, and development through tax-exempt or low-interest financing are commonly associated with these facilities.

Congregate Housing

Congregate housing appeals to the senior who is less active and who has begun to view household upkeep as a burden. Although the age of congregate residents ranges from 65 to 85, the average age tends to be toward the higher end of that range. Congregate facilities often draw from the population of the recently widowed. One of the new forms of elderly housing developed in the 1970s, congregate housing aims to provide more amenities than facilities for independent retirees, without substantially impinging on a senior's sense of independence and without offering any medical care or daily living assistance. Congregate apartments omit the expenses and management headaches that often accompany the health care function provided at continuum-of-care facilities.

Congregate housing is capable of serving a wide range of incomes, and is built by both for-profit and nonprofit firms. Rents at for-profit facilities can range from $700 to $2,500 per month, double to triple standard apartment rents. Rents at nonprofit projects are either minimal or set as a percentage, typically 30%, of a resident's income. Most recently developed congregate units are rentals, although condominiums and cooperatives have been popular. This form of housing is also known as an adult congregate living facility (ACLF), rental retirement housing, or senior retirement center. Today an estimated 300 rental congregate projects exist in the United States, providing about 40,000 units.

Congregate housing is characterized by its services. These include meal service (although residents generally have their own kitchens as well), housekeeping, and linen service, all of which are comparable to the amenities offered by resort hotels. Other services geared toward the specific needs of seniors include extensive recreational and social activities, transportation to shopping and cultural centers, security systems, and emergency call buttons.

The number of units in a congregate facility ranges from 50 to 450. One- and two-bedroom units seem to be the most popular. The facility is usually a single compact building, from two to ten stories tall. Today's developers, however, favor projects of two or three stories. The self-contained complex usually has common areas in the project core for dining and recreational activities. Internal recreation and social facilities include lounges, TV and game rooms, libraries, exercise facilities, chapels, and large social rooms. Beauty shops, convenience stores, drug stores, and coffee shops may also operate in this area. Outdoor recreational facilities are less common in congregate projects, and those provided are minimal compared with retirement communities. Congregate centers often provide gardening plots and shuffleboard courts.

Food service is often the most crucial feature used in marketing a congregate facility. Project developers often go all out to create an elegant, spacious dining area with a restaurant atmosphere. Most centers require that a tenant eat at least one daily meal in the dining hall.

To meet the health care needs of residents, some congregate facilities are affiliated with a nursing home or have an optional home care program. Most offer at least wellness programs such as exercise classes, diets, and lectures. Another frequently offered program is health monitoring by a visiting nurse or doctor. Some centers contract to provide an on-site, part-time nurse or are built on property located in close proximity to a nursing home or hospital.

The facilities and features described above are typical of the luxury or "high-end" development marketed to middle-income and wealthy seniors. Developers will often ask high rents because of the high quality of construction and the amenities offered. It has been observed that, to date, almost all developers interested in congregate senior housing have targeted their proposed projects at the affluent elderly. Despite this fact, a large number of nonprofit or "low-end" congregate developments exist which were built with low-interest government funding in the 1960s and 1970s. These facilities generally provide a smaller package of amenities in a less attractive environment. However, many low-end congregate developments are comparable in quality to those designed for the affluent elderly. These facilities typically have very long waiting lists, because rents can be limited by government regulations to below-market levels or to 30% of a resident's income. Often, potential tenants can shield income or assets to meet income ceiling requirements.

Continuum-of-Care Facilities

The continuum-of-care facility is the most complex type of senior housing option to build and manage. Providing health care on the premises requires state licensing and greatly complicates the financial management of the facility. However, the range of services and living styles offered by these projects can appeal to a wider market than other forms of senior housing.

The continuum-of-care facility can be considered a blend of real estate and medical insurance. The basic premise of the original continuum-of-care facility

22

—the lifecare center—was to ease the worry of seniors who feared they would become sick in old age and would be unable to pay for treatment. Even today, half of all nursing home costs are paid for out-of-pocket, and 15% of health-care costs come from a senior's personal finances. Insurance companies pay for only 1% of the costs at nursing homes. Today, as hospitals attempt to cut costs by placing patients in the more cost-effective skilled nursing facilities, seniors are left with a real fear that they may not be able to provide for themselves in the future. The concept of a lifecare facility is a way of assuaging that fear.

The continuum-of-care concept began in the 1960s and 1970s with lifecare facilities, which were almost always run by nonprofit groups. Because several of these facilities ran into financial problems in the late 1970s, this sector of the elderly housing market has changed. For-profit ventures are taking a larger role in new developments, and the newer facilities have varied fee and financing structures, such as endowments, pay-for-service arrangements, or refundable memberships. They are usually referred to as "continuing care retirement centers," or CCRCs.

With lifecare facilities, a new resident pays a large entrance fee, ranging from $5,000 to $500,000, plus a monthly maintenance fee, with the assurance that he or she can live in that facility permanently and receive health care when needed at the same location. CCRCs offer a less complete insurance policy. They usually provide health care on a fee-for-service basis or contract with a nearby hospital or nursing home.

The CCRC or lifecare resident usually does not obtain a deed to the real property. The entry or endowment fee guarantees a resident the right of occupancy and certain guarantees of health care. In the past, the entry endowment fee was either nonrefundable or partially refundable to a current resident or their estate after an amortization period ranging from one to 10 years. Today, most CCRCs offer a refundable percentage (50% to 90%) plus, in some cases, a percentage of any appreciation in endowment levels.

There are somewhere between 400 and 600 continuum-of-care facilities in the United States, housing about 100,000 people. The number of these facilities has doubled in the last 10 years. The typical model, aimed at upper-income seniors, houses from 200 to 400 people and is laid out in a campus-type environment with a noninstitutional appearance. Most facilities have three segments of housing: independent living units, in cottages, apartments, townhouses, or rooms; congregate-care sections for those needing personal care or help with minor ambulatory problems; and the infirmary or nursing facility for the frailest residents. Admittance to these continuum-of-care facilities requires a legally binding contract, combined with a health requirement. The average age of new entrants is approximately 75 years.

Continuum-of-care facilities offer the same types of services and amenities as congregate centers: a dining hall and meals, housekeeping, security, games and activity rooms, and social events are all typically provided. The extra ingredient is the provision of health care. As with congregate facilities, the range of quality and cost in CCRCs can vary widely from the older, minimum-fee, church-related, nonprofit facility to the ultra-deluxe, for-profit, highly expensive facility. Most of the newly developed facilities have been targeted toward the affluent elderly.

Care Facilities

For a large percentage of the elderly, the need for health care is acute. Among the elderly in the 80-to-85-year-old bracket living on their own, health care is the dominant concern. To answer this need, a wide variety of care facilities have evolved.

Skilled nursing facilities, intermediate nursing facilities, and board and care homes are more a form of health care than shelter, designed to aid the elderly who can no longer take care of themselves. These facilities provide less intensive care than that offered by a general acute-care hospital. Acute-care hospitals are now finding that many of the elderly in their care could live more inexpensively in convalescent homes. In 1984, the elderly spent 21% of their health care expenditures on nursing homes, a figure that is expected to rise. A renewed interest in these facilities by the health industry and developers has led to housing with a new twist: luxury nursing homes. The largest nursing home firm, Beverly Enterprises of Pasadena, California, has 78 luxury homes among its total of 911 facilities.

However, just as hospitals have been found to be unnecessary for some seniors, nursing homes have been found to be unnecessary for others. It has been estimated that anywhere from 15% to 40% of nursing home residents do not need to be there. Many of these residents, it has been argued, could live more independently on a lower rung of the senior care ladder, perhaps in a congregate or CCRC environment.

Skilled nursing facilities or SNFs are operated under the guidance of a licensed administrator. Licensed nurses and certified nursing assistants provide around-the-clock nursing care, including physical, occupational, and other special therapies. Other staff typically include a registered dietitian, a certified activity director, and a director of staff development and education. Nursing-home care is one step below that provided at a general acute-care hospital. The average nursing home resident is an 81-year-old widow, placed in the home by her children, who will stay there for an average of 597 days.

Intermediate care facilities or ICFs are for those elderly who need some nursing and supportive medical care, but not the intensive or continuous care that is provided by an SNF. ICF care is generally less institutional in atmosphere than SNF care and is targeted toward those with functional limitations who require supervision and medical care. The facilities are staffed by licensed and certified personnel.

Both of these facilities are commonly known as nursing homes. The nursing home is a setting for the chronically ill, providing services to patients whose average length of stay is 30 days or longer. This care is paid for privately or through government programs such as Medicare and state-administered Medicaid subsidies. Although a long-term care facility may have a specific license, some beds within that facility may be certified to offer different services. For example, while operating under a skilled nursing license, a facility also may provide services for patients with developmental disabilities or long-term mental illnesses such as Alzheimer's disease.

Residential care facilities or RCFs—also called personal care facilities, retirement hotels, rest homes, or board and care homes—must be licensed in most states. They provide a supportive environment to those who wish to live in a congregate setting. RCF administrators suggest that semiprivate, two-bedroom living promotes interaction and helps avoid psychological atrophy. Generally, all meals are provided and nonmedical help and supervision are also available for many daily functions. RCFs provide personal care programs that include aid in eating, walking, dressing, and other daily activities. Most residents of RCFs are ambulatory and in good overall health, though they do require occasional medical and personal aid. RCF care is paid for privately or through government programs such as supplemental security income subsidies (SSI) for qualifying seniors.

All three types of care facilities usually offer social, recreational, or educational activities, although the quantity and quality of these programs can vary greatly. The quality of medical attention and therapy can also differ significantly from project to project.

4

Design Considerations

Much of the difficulty in developing retirement housing lies in tailoring that project to the special needs and desires of its future residents. This is crucial, however, to the final success of the project, and it pays to invest the necessary time, money, and expertise into the planning and design process. Because of the segmented nature of the elderly market, attempts to appeal to a wide variety of seniors can backfire. Many healthy, active seniors may prefer living in a development without grab bars and emergency call buttons, which can give a project an institutional feeling. These seniors may be uncomfortable with the idea of living with frail and nonambulatory elderly residents, because they do not want to be reminded that they could suffer the same disabilities. On the other hand, frailer seniors may not want to pay for a complex's extensive recreational facilities that they will not use.

Using Focus Groups

The developer of an elderly project should identify the slice of the senior market for which the development is targeted and communicate it clearly to the architect. A preliminary design and target market can be drawn up with the aid of an experienced market analyst, the architect, the sales manager, the project manager, and an expert in the geriatrics field should use information provided by regional demographic analyses and a study of competitive projects in the area. Schematic designs for the project can then be presented to a focus consumer group of about 10 or 12 people. The focus group is a way of testing the market at a very early stage and getting a more concrete idea of the needs and desires of future residents. In addition, the group can become a base of community support for the project in the zoning process and marketing campaign to follow. Among the issues on which focus groups can shed light are the overall building type and layout, the design of common areas, and unit layout and amenities.

Focus groups consulted in past projects have raised a number of relevant concerns. For example, a common complaint of elderly housing residents and focus group members is that projects do not provide enough storage space. Also, focus group members often encourage builders to provide adequate common space for socializing and emphasize good construction quality. The Color Design Art Company of Pacific Palisades, California, surveyed people over 65 about the design features they would prefer in a new home. Seniors were asked to rank each amenity on a scale of 1 (not very important) to 5 (very important). Results of this survey are shown in Table 4.1.

Table 4.1. Design Features Favored by Seniors

Ranked on a scale of 1 (not very important) to 5 (very important)	
High energy efficiency	4.65
Extra storage space	4.61
Lots of natural light	4.23
Extra shelves for books and collectibles	4.18
Large master bedroom	4.09
Master bath with tub and shower stall	3.96
Yard that requires little maintenance	3.78
Large kitchen	3.75
Large living room	3.72
Breakfast nook in kitchen	3.70
Many windows	3.68
Home without stairs	3.44
Fireplace in the living room	3.34
Master bedroom separated from other bedrooms	3.17
Outdoor area for gardening	3.11
Nearby recreational facilities	2.55
Living with people your own age	2.52

SOURCE: Survey by the Color Design Art Company, Pacific Palisades, Calif. Reported in *Real Estate Leasing Report* (June 1986).

Another way of testing the hypothetical project is to conduct an extensive presale campaign before and during construction. The sponsor can get an even more concrete idea of consumer preferences if sales staff are encouraged to relay consumer reaction back to the sponsor. Preferences discovered during the sales process can be used to adjust the project's unit mix or to add certain services, facilities, or unit features.

Depending on the population to be served, the project design will emphasize either activity and independence or a fragile blend designed to foster independence while supplying needed supports. These planning goals will influence the project's location, its exterior construction and landscaping, the allocation of its square footage, and its particular interior design elements.

Location

Location, always a concern in real estate, is even more crucial in the elderly housing field. Because seniors are often less ambulatory than younger adults, they tend to spend more of their time in the neighborhood surrounding their dwelling. The elderly need a neighborhood that provides them with goods, services, entertainment, care, and safety. Not only must the site objectively meet these requirements, the facility's neighborhood must also have the reputation of meeting these requirements. Of course, most neighborhoods cannot meet them all, but the more services and amenities found in the neighborhood, the fewer the developer will be required to provide on site.

Perhaps the most difficult issue when choosing a project site is weighing the benefits of a safe, quiet neighborhood against the increased land costs and the benefits of accessibility to nearby services and activities. The safest neighborhoods tend to be exclusive, spacious, and park-like, and provide an attractive atmosphere as well as protection from crime and violence. However, these neighborhoods are often far away from shops and health facilities and many times lack access to a public transportation network to compensate for the distance. Although some seniors will maintain the independence of their own automobile, most will rely on public transportation or a project's own van service for mobility. An exclusive neighborhood also denies seniors the pleasure of observing the events and activities around them. Studies show that many elderly like to live close to an area where "things happen."

The sponsor should therefore balance a concern for safety, lack of congestion, and crime-free living with the benefits of a lively area. Some of the most important factors in a project's location are proximity to health facilities and hospitals, stores, banks, churches, social services, cultural centers, and friends and relatives. The nearness of health care facilities in particular is essential to many prospective residents, and marketing the facility will be more difficult if a skilled nursing facility or hospital is not a short drive away. A nearby hospital also alleviates the need for extensive in-house health services. Some congregate projects are built on land adjacent to a hospital or skilled nursing facility to provide complementary medical services. Because of federal financing regulations requiring many hospitals and nursing homes to purchase adjacent lands for future expansion, nearby land is sometimes readily available for development.

Other considerations in the location of retirement housing include finding an area with a substantial number of elderly and a site with a minimal amount of competing facilities. The typical neighborhood for a senior project lies between the city's commercial districts and its low-density residential zones, in a buffer area that is usually zoned for high-density residential land use. These buffer zones will generally be close to main thoroughfares, public transportation, and shopping centers. These areas are often devoted to mixed uses and to high-density apartment buildings catering to middle-class and affluent residents.

In some ways, the project's location influences its design. Elderly housing is built everywhere—in cities, in suburbs, and in rural areas. Those projects sited in rural or suburban regions tend to be larger and less dense, reflecting the greater affordability of land. Nonurban facilities may also be larger because of a need to provide certain in-house services that are not available within a reasonable distance. But even urban sites tend to be relatively large to accommodate a lower-density design and more extensive landscaping.

Murata Outland Associates, an architectural and planning firm located in Denver, has devised an informal site evaluation checklist, shown in Figure 4.1, which can be used to assist in the evaluation of specific sites.

Figure 4.1.   Site Evaluation Checklist

1. Site services available:
Gas	Yes___(3)		No___(0)
Electricity	Yes___(3)		No___(0)
Water	Yes___(3)		No___(0)
Sewer	Yes___(3)		No___(0)
Telephone	Yes___(3)		No___(0)

2. Vehicular access to site:
   - From quiet residential street ___(5)
   - From secondary commercial street ___(3)
   - From busy primary artery ___(1)

3. Property zoning:
   - Zoned for elderly housing ___(5)
   - Can be rezoned for elderly housing ___(3)

4. Fire and police protection proximity:
   - 0-1 mile ___(5)
   - 1-5 miles ___(3)
   - 5-10 miles ___(1)
   - Does not exist ___(0)

5. Emergency health care proximity:
   - 0-1 mile ___(5)
   - 1-5 miles ___(3)
   - 5-10 miles ___(1)
   - Does not exist ___(0)

6. Full service hospital proximity:
   - 0-1 mile ___(5)
   - 1-5 miles ___(3)
   - 5-10 miles ___(1)
   - Greater than 10 miles ___(0)

7. Participation of medical facility in project:
   Yes___(5)   No___(0)

8. Degree of neighborhood safety and security:
   - Very safe ___(5)
   - Average ___(3)
   - Security required ___(1)

9. Cultural facility proximity: theater, library, museum, etc.
   - 0-5 blocks ___(5)
   - 1/2-1 mile ___(3)
   - 1-5 miles ___(1)
   - 5-10 miles ___(0)

10. Religious facility proximity:
   - 0-5 blocks ___(5)
   - 1/2-1 mile ___(3)
   - 1-5 miles ___(1)
   - 5-10 miles ___(0)

Figure 4.1. Site Evaluation Checklist—continued

11. Convenience shopping proximity: bank, drugstore, cleaners, deli, etc.

0-5 blocks	_____(5)
½-1 mile	_____(3)
1-5 miles	_____(1)
5-10 miles	_____(0)

12. Parks and recreation facility proximity:

0-5 blocks	_____(5)
½-1 mile	_____(3)
1-5 miles	_____(1)
5-10 miles	_____(0)

13. Major shopping mall proximity:

0-5 miles	_____(5)
5-10 miles	_____(3)
10-20 miles	_____(1)

14. Public transportation access point:

At site	_____(5)
2 blocks	_____(3)
5 blocks	_____(1)
Does not exist	_____(0)

15. Surrounding property value:

Comparable	_____(5)
Lower	_____(3)
Higher	_____(1)

16. Project design and compatibility with surrounding neighborhood (Example: Highrise in neighborhood of single-family bungalows not compatible):

Yes_____(5)   No_____(0)

17. Completion of market study and demographic analysis of site:

Yes_____(5)   No_____(0)

18. Nearest similar facility:

5-10 miles	_____(5)
1-5 miles	_____(3)
0-1 mile	_____(1)

Scoring: Maximum Score = 100 points

85 to 100	Excellent	Should appeal to wide market.
70 to 85	Good site	Depending on negatives, may have slightly limited market range.
55 to 70	Average site	Need to carefully evaluate negatives. May have limited marketability.
0 to 55	Below average	May be more risks than necessary. Get several additional opinions.

This study has been formulated for the primary purpose of encouraging a thorough analysis of any potential site being considered for an elderly housing project. It includes major elements which will have a definite impact, negatively or positively, on the future success of the project under consideration. In all cases, a site analysis, market study, and demographic study by an accredited and recognized consulting firm is highly recommended.

Use of this checklist is solely for analysis purposes and is not intended to be used as the basis for business or development decisions. Murata Outland Associates will not be held liable for decisions made based solely on this survey.

SOURCE: Murata Outland Associates, Denver. Reprinted with permission.

Exterior Design

Designing the exterior or interior of a senior housing project demands an emphasis on certain goals that are significantly different from those embodied in traditional housing. Seniors shopping for a new place to live are highly discriminating: not only are they often experienced homebuyers, but they are aware that this may be the last housing decision they make. They want to be able to step into the front hall of a development and feel that it is warm, secure, and supportive, while at the same time youthful and lively in atmosphere.[1]

Design plays a crucial role in creating the quality and image of a project. Lobbies, lounges, and exterior hallways provide the most important first impressions of a facility's atmosphere and should emphasize the home-like aspects of the project over the institutional. The development should have an image that is younger than the market group being targeted. For example, a recent trend in elderly housing is the construction of "theme" retirement centers. These developments are designed to inspire nostalgia, and are constructed and landscaped to create a "turn of the century," "farming community," or "English country inn" atmosphere.

An elderly project is often constructed of less expensive but easy-to-maintain materials, such as stucco or masonite-based hardboard. Residents will often prefer to see their money go into recreational amenities or services. As it is, construction costs will already be higher because of the special features designed into the project such as oversized doorways and reinforced bathroom walls, and because of safety requirements such as a sprinkler system. Many states require the use of stronger and more durable construction materials if the facility is to include health care services such as those found in a CCRC. Because most developers of new projects have targeted their complex to the affluent elderly, the overall construction quality at most recently built congregate senior developments is similar to other high-end apartment or condominium developments.

To bring a part of the outside world into the development, the exterior areas of the project should be lush and well landscaped. The greenery can present a pleasant scene for a senior who may spend most of his or her time near home. The objective of a landscaping plan for a facility surrounded by contrasting development is to create a self-contained environment, buffered and secure from outside activity without being confining or institutional. Landscaping can include a pond or other aquatic element, an exercise course, extensive walkways, or a variety of gardens and flowers. There may be additional psychological benefits if the sponsor sets aside plots for the amateur gardeners in the project, because this allows residents to exercise an element of control over their environment.

The landscaping should also buffer housing units from another important exterior element: the parking lot or garage. Because many seniors do not drive,

---

[1] For a more comprehensive treatment of elderly housing design, see Diane Y. Carstens, *Site Planning and Design for the Elderly* (New York: Van Nostrand Reinhold, 1985).

sponsors are inclined to offer fewer parking spaces. Parking ratios usually range from one space per four units to one space per unit. Residents of an elderly project sometimes complain, however, when they have not been provided with enough parking. Many residents will own cars that they seldom drive, and others like to know that there is plenty of room for their guests' automobiles. Other concerns about parking include the security of the lot, the adequacy of lighting at night, and its proximity to dwelling units and the central lobby. Finally, developers must gauge city officials' acceptance of lower-than-average parking requirements.

Tables 4.2 through 4.4 illustrate ranges and relationships between the sizes of key areas of congregate, CCRC, and residential care projects. These statistics show significant differences in overall development size, unit mix, and allocation of gross building area.

Table 4.2. Square Footage Statistics, Congregate Rental Facility

Facility	Number of Units	Total Living Area	Common Area	Gross Building Area	Land Area	Floor to Area Ratio	Parking Spaces	Parking Spaces/ Unit
A	174	104,700	60,160	164,860	322,344	0.51	90	.52
B	165	137,250	37,550	174,800	239,580	0.62	150	.91
C	150	99,168	53,300	152,468	191,664	0.80	92	.61
D	110	41,535	39,421	80,956	32,250	2.51	41	.37
E	158	126,640	107,531	234,171	84,000	2.79	168	1.06
F	178	112,080	43,793	155,873	239,850	0.65	73	.41
G	234	204,156	100,644	304,800	345,430	0.88	139	.59
H	196	142,740	83,940	226,680	392,040	0.58	128	.65
I	166	107,750	36,901	144,651	207,781	0.70	117	.60
J	206	119,768	41,482	161,250	416,000	0.39	206	1.00
Average	174	119,579	60,472	180,051	247,067	1.04	120	.67

Table 4.3. Square Footage Statistics, CCRCs

Facility	Congregate Apts.	Residential Care	Skilled Nursing	Total Living Area	Common Area	Gross Building Area	Land Area	Floor to Area Ratio	Parking Spaces	Parking Spaces/ Unit
A	124	0	36 units 59 beds	88,400	57,554	145,954	272,686	0.54	126	.69
B	180	50 units 89 beds	32 units 50 beds	113,042	48,458	161,500	448,189	0.36	216	.68
C	114	36 units 36 beds	60 units 99 beds	107,193	64,361	171,554	302,742	0.57	143	.68
D	207	16 units 16 beds	0	224,663	207,199	431,862	86,252	5.01	178	.80
E	196	0	59 units 128 beds	176,912	43,640	220,552	886,315	0.25	243	.75
Average	164	34 units 47 beds	47 units 84 beds	142,042	84,242	226,284	399,237	1.35	181	.72

Table 4.4. Square Footage Statistics, Residential Care Facility

Facility	Units	Beds	Total Living Area	Common Area	Gross Building Area	Land Area	Floor to Area Ratio	Parking Spaces	Parking Spaces/ Bed
A	52	94	14,040	30,508	44,548	33,000	1.35	31	.33
B	32	70	15,028	4,972	20,000	60,000	0.33	43	.61
C	25	50	8,458	11,527	19,985	61,855	3.10	35	.70
D	14	28	1,763	3,944	5,707	12,240	2.15	15	.54
E	9	15	2,215	4,565	6,780	6,000	0.89	12	.80
Average	26	51	8,301	11,103	19,404	34,619	1.56	27	.53

As these tables show, most projects contain from 120 to 250 units. One-bedroom units are by far the most popular form of housing and sponsors are beginning to include a much smaller percentage of studio and alcove apartments in their projects. Two-bedroom apartments are popular with affluent couples, who will often use the second room as a guest room, work room, or study. Units tend to become smaller as the facility moves toward the dependent end of the housing spectrum, with less active people requiring less space. Average size ranges for housing are as follows: studios, 250 to 550 square feet; alcoves, 400 to 750 square feet; one-bedroom units, 600 to 1,000 square feet; and two-bedroom units, 800 to 1,200 square feet. Prototypical unit designs are shown in Figure 4.2.

Interior Design

Interior design is often quite specific to the needs of seniors. Much of the design features are intended to allow the elderly to "age in place," so that their limitations do not exceed the capacity of the dwelling. Many seniors decide to leave their home after realizing their diminished ability to take care of the house and take care of themselves in that setting. Through design, the environment of elderly housing projects can foster a senior's independence.

Suggested interior designs for congregate and CCRC facilities include

- Well-lit, extra-wide corridors and doorways to accommodate wheelchairs. The recommended width is between six and eight feet.
- Elevators, with doors that close slowly, rather than stairs
- Designs that avoid other possible barriers such as high thresholds, multiple-level units, and thick carpets
- Handrails along corridors
- Chairs with taller seats for public spaces and individual units
- Lighting and use of color that are sensitive to possible eye problems. Lighting that causes glare or multiple shadows can also cause confusion for tenants, while the use of brighter, more distinct colors can define the difference between a wall and the floor for poor eyesight.
- Lever handles on doors to provide an easy grip for arthritic hands

Figure 4.2. Unit Designs

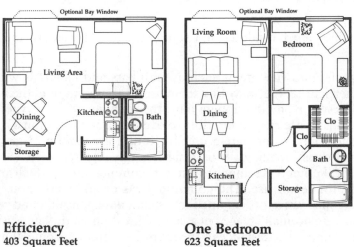

Efficiency
403 Square Feet

One Bedroom
623 Square Feet

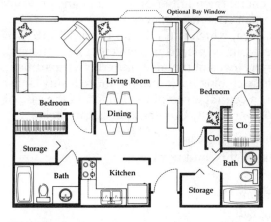

Two Bedroom
957 Square Feet

SOURCE: *Understanding Elderly Housing* (Denver: Murata Outland Associates). Reprinted with permission.

- Individually controlled heaters
- A communication system to the central offices
- Electrical wall outlets placed at waist height rather than near the floor
- Grab bars or reinforcement of bathroom walls for future installation of grab bars, if needed
- Nonslip floors
- Lower kitchen cabinets. Where possible, pantries are preferred over additional cabinets.

- Controls on ranges and ovens at the front, rather than the rear, of the appliance
- Ample storage space
- Double-paned windows and sound-attenuated walls to mute exterior noises

Seniors sometimes view items such as grab bars and handrails with distaste, despite the fact that they may find them useful at present or in the near future. For this reason, many developers limit the number of these types of design specifications or use elegant interiors to overcome an institutional appearance. A developer can also prepare a unit for future installation of grab bars and other aids by reinforcing walls or designing movable items.

The focal point of a senior project is its common areas, which are uniquely developed for senior use. The common areas of an elderly housing project contain administrative offices, mailboxes, and dining, health, and recreational spaces, and are normally placed in a central location on the site, easily accessible from all units. The distance to the lobby is a common complaint of project residents, but in general the number of units and an allowance for landscaping will mandate a certain stretch of space.

The common area, which can take up from 20% to 40% of the project's gross building area, can be placed in the center of a triangular or rectangular layout of units; at the locus of tentacle-like arms of apartments; at one end of a project, with units stretching back into the more lushly landscaped sections of a property; around a central green or garden; or, in the case of a self-contained high-rise, on the lower levels. Common areas can include:

- Lobby with seating areas
- Fireplaces, skylights, and terrace
- Lounge
- Public restrooms
- Main dining hall
- Private dining area
- Kitchen
- Administrative offices
- Mailroom
- Storage spaces
- Laundry room
- Chapel
- Garage
- Medical office and nurses' area
- Commercial spaces:
    Barber and beauty shop
    Drug and prescription store
    Gift shop

Snack bar
General store
Branch bank
Travel agency
- Recreational spaces:
Meeting rooms
Social/recreational hall
Sewing room
Arts and crafts room
Exercise room, spa, and sauna
Game room
Library
Movie screening room
TV room
Greenhouse
Indoor pool

Common area design is a function of site area, cost, resident characteristics, and the imagination of the project architect.

5

Management

Management has become so important to the ultimate success or failure of a senior project that most institutional lenders now require a developer to hire a professional management team for any facility. Many lending institutions expect the developer to have identified a manager before the search for financing even begins. Lenders recognize that good management spells the difference between a high attrition rate and a group of stable, satisfied residents. The developer of a project is creating not only real estate, but also a program of services and even a lifestyle—in general, a warm, friendly, supportive environment that will engage the resident and encourage a 10- or 20-year stay there. Management is the key to the creation of that environment.

Elderly housing management is not comparable to the management of standard housing projects. It requires much more in the way of social skills, interaction, and intervention. The manager of an elderly project is a combination of organizer, cheerleader, therapist, and caregiver. Although most developers stress the noninstitutional quality of their retirement projects, the concepts of care, support, and protection are essential to many of these facilities. Seniors may fall ill, become isolated and antisocial, or need help with housework, eating, or dressing. Aside from facilities that cater to the youngest members of the senior market, most elderly projects will house seniors with these types of frailties, and a manager must be able to deal effectively with them. Because of these specialized skills and considerations, qualified elderly housing management is currently in high demand and should remain so for many years.

Recognizing this demand, industry associations offer seminars and publications on the operation and management of senior housing. These groups include the National Association of Senior Living Industries, the American Association of Homes for the Aged, the American Association of Retired Persons, and the National Council on Aging. Publications such as the *Housing the Elderly Report*, published by CD Publications of Silver Springs, Maryland, provide a monthly forum for a discussion of day-to-day management issues and problems.

A project's management should be under consideration from the first day of the development process. Because managers will be coping with the physical aspects of a project for many years, the sponsor would be wise to include a management representative during project design. This representative can envision the project in use in the future and can identify potential inefficiencies in design and layout.

When considering what type of management to employ, a sponsor has a number of options. To handle management duties, the owner of the project can hire a professional management team for a specific service (security, grounds maintenance, housekeeping, or food service) or hire an individual or a nonprofit management board or committee. Many lenders prefer to see one professional management group in charge of operating a project, because this type of arrangement can reduce costs and operate with greater efficiency. Lastly, a sponsor can opt for turn-key management, where a professional firm trains the sponsor's staff for two or three years, gradually turning over control to the sponsor. When choosing a management team, the sponsor should look for a proven track record in elderly housing management, a sensitivity to fiscal concerns and social issues, and a system of day-to-day operating procedures.

Administration

Staffing

Although a bare-bones elderly facility with a minimum of services can get along with a staff of three—a manager, an assistant manager, and a custodian —the newer, multiservice facilities are labor-intensive. The sizeable staff should be well trained and, most importantly, staff members must understand their role as caregivers and representatives of the facility as a whole. They must be capable of treating residents with respect and consideration, and should be able to look out for the well-being of residents, recognizing any changes that might signal danger.

According to the accounting firm of Laventhol & Horwath, a typical CCRC, containing about 200 apartments, a 60-bed nursing center, and a 25-bed personal care unit, would need a staff of about 100 persons. That would include about six personal care employees, 33 administrative and medical personnel in the nursing center, and 23 people working in food service. An executive director, an assistant executive director, and a full-time residential support staff encompassing administrative, housekeeping, transportation, maintenance, and security functions would make up another third of the staff. Community volunteers often supplement the salaried staff in a senior facility. Obviously, less sophisticated projects can be managed with fewer employees. Offering on-site medical care greatly increases the required number of staff workers. The industry average is one employee for every two to three residents.

At the heart of the management staff is the management team, comprised of the executive manager, the management agent, the property supervisor, and the resident manager. When selecting the management team, the sponsor should weigh the individual's leadership and management qualities, knowledge of local community services, knowledge of the aging process, and ability to understand and empathize with seniors.

The executive manager heads the team, setting policies and overseeing the rental agent and all staff. Normally, the executive manager is not permanently located at any one specific development. The responsibility for day-to-day operations and expenses belongs to the site-based management agent or project administrator, who also handles contracting for services from outside firms. Responsibility for the physical site itself belongs to the property supervisor, who must enforce policy, direct staff work, monitor costs, and obtain materials and other resources for maintenance-related services and activities. The property supervisor and staff are expected to interact with residents and be alert for social or medical problems. Finally, the resident manager or social services/medical director is the closest tie to the residents, making certain that facilities and services meet the needs of residents.

Basic Management Services

Although the management of elderly housing involves a vast array of specialized services, at its core remain the basic services common to all housing facilities. These include

- Processing applications to rent or purchase a unit
- Collecting rent and terminating tenancy
- Maintaining the budget and cost accounting
- Cleaning, repair, and maintenance
- Developing job descriptions and schedules
- Inspection and upkeep

More recent elderly housing projects couple these common duties with those more akin to social services, requiring a much greater input on the part of management as the facility takes over more of its residents' responsibilities. The management of housekeeping, dining services, medical services, and social services will be discussed more fully at the end of the chapter.

In-house Relations

An important component of successful management is attitude. Misguided managers sometimes take on a "parent" role or a condescending manner with residents. Residents are not there simply to be managed. It should never be forgotten that a facility is the residents' home, and services and amenities are designed to please them. Although they may be suffering from physical or even mental limitations, they demand the same respect as other adults. Their comments and criticisms should be carefully considered, and, although they may need help at times, they should be allowed to live in a way that maximizes their independence. Because of this, the manager's role can be a careful and very difficult balancing act. An important industry maxim to remember is, "The elderly are no different from you or me; they are only more experienced."

A number of management problems are characteristic of elderly housing. A manager of nonelderly housing usually does not need to worry about the residents isolating themselves and becoming lonely or depressed, but this problem is common within the elderly population. Up to 85% of the residents may be women, many widowed. They may be experiencing a new-found loneliness. Similarly, elderly men tend to withdraw and avoid facility-run social events. This isolation, coupled with fears of growing old, getting sick, or dying, is particularly common among seniors.

Another problem is that the residents, often living alone, can trip or suffer a sudden physical attack without being discovered in time to receive emergency treatment. Residents may also suffer a slow deterioration of mental or physical capabilities. If they feel they could be asked to leave as their condition deteriorates, they may isolate themselves to escape notice, exacerbating the medical problems. Very often, the physical conditions that seniors attribute to old age can actually be treated, but if the condition is left unaddressed, it can cause permanent disabilities.

A well-trained and alert service staff can protect against these dangers. Housekeepers, maintenance staff, and security personnel interact with residents while pursuing their daily routines. Their schedules and locations can be coordinated so that they get to know residents and can play a supportive and communicative role, reporting any physical or emotional changes that may require treatment or referring a counselor to a lonely or depressed resident.

To establish relations with residents and address complaints, the manager often establishes a resident committee or has a spokesperson appointed or elected to meet regularly with management. Bulletins, memos, and newsletters also facilitate resident-manager communication.

Acceptance of New Residents

Because new congregate and lifecare centers are often in high demand, and because many facilities are specifically oriented to a particular age or capability group within the elderly population, most facilities set up an intricate screening process for potential residents. This process should be standardized and include a clear explanation of the project's established exit criteria as well, so that a new resident will be aware of the health and support services the project can provide and at what point a resident must leave. Table 5.1 provides a suggested checklist to help identify a potential resident's independence level.

Table 5.1. Independent Living Capabilities, 20 Critical Factors

Independent

1. Able to prepare adequate meals independently. Eats without assistance.
2. Maintains home alone or with occasional help with heavy work.
3. Is mobile without any aids. Can walk six to eight blocks and climb stairs without assistance.
4. Toilet-cares for self at toilet completely. No incontinence.
5. Medications—is responsible for taking medications in correct dosages at correct times without assistance.
6. Has little or no difficulty with time, place, person orientation (Goldfarb-Kahn-Pollack test).
7. Able to participate fully in planning and exercises good judgment in decision making or substantially intact —capable of participating in planning and decision making with minor dependence on others.
8. Apparently free of anxiety, depression, phobias, or paranoia, or symptoms may be present in mild form but do not significantly hinder daily functioning.
9. Use of drugs or alcohol is not abusive.
10. Is aware of and practices routine safety measures without reminders or teaching assistance.
11. Obtains own groceries and other items needed for daily living.
12. Manages financial matters independently (budgets, writes and cashes checks, pays rent and bills, goes to bank, collects and keeps track of income).
13. Travels independently on public transportation or drives own car or arranges own travel via taxi but does not otherwise use public transportation.
14. Bathing: bathes self (tub, shower, sponge bath) without help.
15. Dressing: dresses, undresses, and selects clothes from own wardrobe with no or very minor assistance.
16. Grooming: neatness, hair, nails, hands, face, clothing. Always neatly dressed, well groomed without assistance.
17. Free of disturbing, disabling character traits or personal habits; grooming and dress reflect good hygiene and interest in personal appearance, or mildly disturbing character traits which would not significantly impair capacity for group living, acceptable personal habits and hygiene.
18. Maintains satisfactory relationships with family, friends, and other residents. May be becoming less active in sustaining them.
19. Is able to speak, hear, read, and write with little or no difficulty.
20. Able to dial and converse over the telephone. Able to look up numbers.

Independent with supportive services

1. Requires health aide, homemaker, family, or friends to prepare adequate meals on periodic or short-term basis. Eats with minor assistance and may be untidy.

2. Performs light daily tasks but cannot maintain acceptable level of cleanliness without chore service, homemaker. Assistance is available and accepted.

3. Is mobile with mechanical aids (wheelchair, cane, crutches, walker, braces) or occasional available assistance. Able to go in and out of wheelchair without assistance.

4. Needs reminders about or minor and occasional assistance with toilet, personal care. May soil or wet while asleep more than once every two weeks.

5. At times confused by medications and requires periodic supervision of dosages. Supervision available and accepted.

6. Has intermittent or moderate confusion in time, place, person orientation.

7. Occasional memory lapses. May have always had limited intellectual capacities. Can participate in planning but may be slow in grasping content or need support from others in decision making.

8. May have mildly disturbing or mildly disabling anxiety, depression, phobias, or paranoia.

9. Is developing a pattern of drug or alcohol abuse. Has not caused disturbances, accepts assistance.

10. Routine safety measures: requires some teaching assistance initially, but functions satisfactorily with no further assistance.

11. Obtains own food and other necessary items with some assistance from others. Assistance is available.

12. Manages some day-to-day purchases but needs help with banking and major purchases. May have or need conservator.

13. Travels on public transportation when assisted by others or travels limited to taxi or automobile with assistance of others. Occasionally requires others to make transportation arrangements for them. Assistance is available.

14. Bathes self with help in getting in and out of tub or shower; or washes face and hands only but cannot bathe rest of body. Accepts available assistance of family, friends, health aide or homemaker to bathe rest of body.

15. Needs moderate assistance in dressing, undressing, and selection of clothes. Assistance is available and accepted.

16. Grooms self adequately with help of hygiene education or assistance. May need moderate assistance on short-term basis. Assistance is available and accepted.

17. Mildly disturbing character traits which are not too disabling. Continues to have interest in appearance and maintains acceptable hygiene with some supervision.

18. May have had adequate interpersonal relationships in the past, but currently shows diminution of interest or minor to moderate problems with this sphere. May require occasional encouragement or stimulation. May be developing a pattern of difficulty with interpersonal relationships, including family and other residents.

19. Is able to speak and hear or read and write. May have moderate difficulty and may use electronic or mechanical aids.

20. Uses phone with difficulty. May only dial a few well-known numbers. May need electronic aid.

Supported living situations required

1. Requires extensive assistance with all meals or refuses to prepare or eat adequate meals. Totally dependent on health aide, homemaker, family, or friends for preparation of adequate meals. Refuses assistance, or assistance is not available.

2. Needs help with all home maintenance tasks. Does not participate in any housekeeping tasks or refuses assistance in maintaining acceptable level of cleanliness, or assistance is not available.

3. Requires extensive assistance on a regular basis to carry out routine living functions—in and out of wheelchair, bed, toilet, or dressing. Refuses assistance, or assistance is not available.

4. Soils or wets while awake more than once a week or has no control over bladder or bowels.

5. Requires daily or excessive supervision of medications for more than short period of time. Refuses supervision, or supervision is not readily available.

6. Severely disoriented in regard to time, place, and person.

7. Requires considerable help from others in planning and decision making. Memory disorientation is sufficient to warrant daily or around-the-clock nursing care and supervision. Totally dependent on others for planning.

8. May have moderate to severe disturbing or disabling anxiety, depression, phobias, or paranoia. Possibility of danger to self and others.

9. Frequently under the influence of drugs or alcohol and displays disruptive behavior. Does not maintain own health and apartment. Refuses assistance.

10. Refuses to practice safety measures or is frequently unaware of normal safety precautions.

11. Cannot or will not obtain food and other necessary items. Refuses assistance, or assistance is not available.

12. Incapable of handling financial matters. Has or needs guardian. Refuses assistance, or assistance is not available.

13. Requires extensive assistance with transportation or help in obtaining transportation for medical or dental appointments. Does not or will not travel, or adequate transportation is not available.

14. Cannot or will not wash self. Refuses assistance, or assistance is not available.

15. Needs major assistance with dressing, and such assistance is not available.

16. Needs regular assistance, or supervision in grooming. Refuses assistance, or assistance is not available.

17. Moderately to severely disturbing character traits. Requires considerable supervision and assistance for personal grooming. Incapable of conforming to socially acceptable standards of personal hygiene. Character traits create severe problems in management.

18. Needs considerable to excessive encouragement or stimulation. Interest and concern with regard to others has diminished. May be unable to maintain more than minimal personal relationship.

19. Has severe impairments of communication faculties. Has excessive difficulty in understanding and being understood. Refuses assistance, or assistance is not available.

20. Does not use telephone, or refuses to have phone even though it is necessary for health and safety.

SOURCE: Rosetta E. Parker, *Housing for the Elderly: The Handbook for Managers* (Chicago: Institute of Real Estate Management, 1984), p. 121. Reprinted with permission.

The screening process normally requires a medical report so that the sponsor can become familiar with the extent of the resident's needs. A new medical report can be required at each lease renewal. Priorities for selection or for placement on the waiting list may include the date of application, the applicant's need, availability of appropriate unit size, and a preferred mix of genders or religious backgrounds. The staff should be familiar with elderly housing options in the area to make referrals and be aware of occasions when another facility may be better suited to the needs of the applicant.

Services

Dining

To guarantee proper nutrition and ease the burden of cooking and washing dishes, congregate facilities and lifecare centers usually provide residents with at least one meal a day. The quality of this meal—both its preparation and presentation—is one of the most critical factors for seniors choosing an elderly facility, and can be a major marketing tool for the project as a whole. The meal is often the primary daily social event for seniors, and a fair or poor meal can add a sour tone to the occasion.

Because of this, developers usually go all out in designing the dining area and in planning meals and presentation. Most facilities aim for a noninstitutional appearance in their dining room, clustering elegant tables for four and often adding linen and quality cutlery. Although most project sponsors use a buffet style of service, some offer waited tables. Projects often serve the day's meals in a European style, with the largest meal of the day around noon and a lighter meal in the evening. Many facilities emphasize variety in their menus while ensuring a proper diet. Special low-cholesterol meals or menus for diabetics are sometimes available. Sponsors unfamiliar with food service management can contract with outside food service operators.

Housekeeping

Both congregate and lifecare facilities provide other services similar to those found at hotels to make life easier for elderly residents. Most provide a weekly housecleaning service and linen service. This is usually included in the monthly rent, but is sometimes assessed on a fee-for-service basis. Occasionally a laundry service will be provided. More often, however, the project simply provides a laundry room, which many times will become a prime social gathering spot for residents.

Medical Services

By far the widest variety in services are directed toward health needs. Because the new types of projects are geared to filling the wide gap between standard housing and full-scale medical facilities, numerous ways have been found to address the health needs of the elderly. Health care services generally fall into one of five categories, listed below in order from least to most intensive.

1. Full independent living, including diet planning
2. Congregate living including full meal and housekeeping services
3. Personal care
4. Intermediate nursing care
5. Skilled nursing care

In addition to meal, housekeeping, and social services, congregate projects often feature educational programs, including health care training such as CPR and the Heimlich maneuver; nutritional information; and some sort of physical conditioning, from organized walks to dance and calisthenics classes. This can be coupled with a mobile unit program to provide checkups, physical therapy, education, personal care, and referrals. Many projects also require an annual physical, eye, and dental checkup.

While they do not provide medical care, congregate facilities sometimes contain separate personal care or "assisted living" units for residents who may need help with daily activities such as bathing, eating, dressing, transportation, or personal hygiene. Personal care units are normally grouped together in one section of the facility. In most states, a facility is required to obtain a license from the state social service agency before providing any type of medical or living assistance service. The range of health-related services available in a congregate environment is illustrated in Table 5.2.

Table 5.2.   On-Site Health-Related Services

Service	Frequency of Provision
On staff, 24-hour nurse	Very rare
On staff, part-time nurse	Increasingly common
Scheduled health monitoring by visiting nurses or doctors	Frequent
Provision of on-site space for use by physicians and other health professionals not on staff	Frequent
Wellness programs (lectures, exercise, special diets, etc.)	Increasingly common

SOURCE: Federal Research Press, *Retirement Housing Report* (October 1986), p. 10.

Lifecare facilities and CCRCs go a step further than congregate centers by providing full medical care. The service, under the supervision of licensed personnel, is designed to meet any subacute medical need that a resident might have. Facilities often have an on-site clinic or infirmary to perform checkups, X-rays, and lab work and to dispense prescriptions. They provide personal care wards and also often make available intermediate or skilled nursing care. Intermediate care includes less intensive and continuous nursing care for those residents with physical or socialization limitations. Skilled nursing care—the highest level available outside the hospital—is offered on a 24-hour basis for those needing constant medical supervision.

In the past, these services were offered on-site by lifecare facilities as part of the entrance package. But increasingly, newer CCRCs are contracting with nearby hospitals, clinics, and skilled nursing facilities to provide off-site services or are charging residents on a fee-for-service basis. This shift is a response to skyrocketing health costs and, because of the unpredictability of demand for the services, is viewed as a more efficient, less risky method of serving residents.

Social Services

One of the most vital aims of elderly housing projects is providing an environment for seniors that encourages social interaction and provides opportunities for meaningful activities. Management should create an atmosphere where it is difficult to lead a listless, isolated life. The varied activities and social services offered at projects include transportation, adult education and workshops, and special counseling, as well as everyday recreation and special events.

Transportation. Buses or vans can be used for regular shopping trips or transportation to health facilities, the Social Security office, the post office, or entertainment centers. Coordinators will often plan special trips for travel or entertainment. Many projects also take advantage of outside services such as Dial-a-Ride or group fair reductions provided by local transit agencies.

Adult education and workshops. Classes can serve both entertainment and goal-oriented functions, offering crafts instruction or preparation for new employment or part-time jobs. Popular subjects include nutrition, budgeting, sewing, and English.

Counseling. The counseling center should be located in a private area where residents can talk without fear of being overheard. This service can address both practical needs—relating to Social Security, work, health insurance, legal, or financial advice—or deal with more intimate subjects that are psychological or spiritual in nature. Centers often encourage local members of the clergy to contact residents or to attend in-house events.

Recreation and events. These range from public-interest or political forums to clubs, skills-exchange workshops, study groups, movies, dances, physical therapy, games, bridge tournaments, and newsletters.

6

Financing

Financing for an elderly housing project can be difficult to acquire. Federal funding for loan programs has been cut back, eliminating much of the nonprofit development activity that, until recently, dominated the market. In the conventional financing arena, many lenders are worried about overbuilding of elderly housing and are unfamiliar with the industry's basic factors, such as the typically extended lease-up period. Yet other conventional lenders are bullish on this market, and a number of tax-exempt or below-market rate options still exist. Generally, builders of elderly housing have been able to turn to one financing mechanism or another to draw funds for their developments.

Table 6.1. Comparison of Financing Programs

Time Span (Months)	Fees	Rate	Preset Restrictions	Amortization Period (Years)	Percent of Project Borrowed	Availability
			Federal programs			
9-12	Points plus legal and printing fees plus application fees[1]	Less than tax-exempt[2]	Charge structure Clientele Building specifications	40	90-100	Severely limited by appropriation
			Tax-exempt borrowings			
4-6	Points plus legal and printing fees	Less than prime	Ownership Additional debt	30	80-100	Depends on purpose of local authority
			Conventional mortgage			
2-4	Points	Prime plus 2 percent	None	15	60	No restrictions on availability

[1] Section 202 does not change any significant fees whatsoever.
[2] Section 202 rates are pegged at 9.25 percent, which has been lower than any other rate.
SOURCE: Matthews E. Ward, "Congregate Living Arrangements: The Financing Option," *Topics in Healthcare Financing* (Spring 1984), p. 34.

The use of various types of financing methods has shifted through time, in response to the economy, interest rate fluctuations, and shifting federal laws and restrictions. For example, before 1960, many lifecare projects built by religious groups were financed through entry fees in combination with donations and endowments.

Conventional Financing

Conventional mortgages have remained a major financing option through the years, although the recession of the early 1980s led to an unwillingness among lenders to finance retirement centers. Since then, conventional loans have become easier to obtain as news about elderly demographics and the success of the new senior housing types has spread through the real estate industry. Mortgage bankers, however, still remain wary about investing in an industry with which they are often unfamiliar. Because elderly housing is not well known, lender perception of the industry varies widely. A recent nationwide lender survey revealed that debt coverage ratios, loan-to-value ratios, financing charges, and due dates for elderly housing loans all differ greatly from lender to lender. This survey will be discussed in detail later in this chapter.

Conventional mortgages remain the quickest method of financing, with a loan application process averaging two to four months. These loans lack the restrictions often contained in government financing programs such as an inclusionary requirement, the prohibition of an entrance fee, or maintenance of a large reserve fund. Conventional loans allow a developer to negotiate a deal that meets his or her needs. Of course, financing costs of conventional loans tend to be higher than government-supported financing.

Among the types of conventional loans available are fixed-interest mortgage loans, lender participation loans, interest-only loans with balloon payments after 10 to 12 years, negative amortization loans, and variable rate mortgage loans. The loan-to-value ratio of conventional mortgages averages about 75% of total project cost for elderly housing, requiring the developer to contribute equity to the project as well. The average interest rate on elderly housing loans in 1986 ranged from 10% to 11.5%, reflecting market conditions.

In considering whether to underwrite a loan, lenders show particular concern about experience, equity, careful planning, and estimates of market demand. Lenders look carefully at the developer's knowledge of the elderly housing industry and its sometimes quirky, shallow market. They want evidence of a proven track record of successful projects, and will study the developer's "deep pockets" for the ability to come up with equity and maintain the project through a long, expensive lease-up period. Most lenders require a sponsor to hire a professional management firm with experience in senior projects, and often ask for a strategic plan for marketing, leasing, service programs, and operation.

Beyond the strengths of the developer, the project itself must be appropriate for a specific market. Most lenders require a professional appraisal and an extensive market or project feasibility study. The latter should address evidence of local demand, service and location issues, competition, and factors of marketability and market penetration. The lender will also look at the adequacy of fees or rents, operating expense estimates, and the reliability of contracting and architectural firms.

If there is difficulty in securing a loan, the project sponsor might consider the possibility of a joint venture with a medical provider or an institutional lender such as an insurance company or pension fund. There can be a substantial cost, namely the partial loss of control and the loss of a large percentage of the project's profit and equity. However, savings and loans and insurance companies see advantages in these types of relationships and may be persuaded to enter into an otherwise unworkable development. As with conventional loans, this type of arrangement allows for a great deal of flexibility for each partner; terms and conditions, equity contributions, and the percentage of profit to be shared can be settled through negotiation. The most standard form of joint venture involves a 50-50 split of costs and profits.

Another method of conventional financing is the formation of limited partnerships. With this method, the investors assume all the risks, and the general partner or operator usually has the option of buying the project after it has been operating more than 10 years and the tax benefits have diminished. A limited partnership can be used in tandem with other financing options to obtain equity, for example, on the roughly 20% of project financing not covered by a conventional mortgage. Recent tax law changes have made syndication arrangements problematic and a less viable alternative. Other joint venture options include an arrangement between a smaller developer who has conceived a project idea and a larger developer with a solid reputation, or a venture between a for-profit developer and a nonprofit organization that brings experience and tax advantages into the partnership.

Tax-Exempt Bond Financing

A popular alternative to conventional financing has been tax-exempt securities, which usually offer a percentage rate averaging about 2 to 2.5 percentage points below taxable market rates because of their nontaxable status. Bonds allow the most flexible loan periods, varying from five to 40 years, and, combined with credit enhancements, offer a definite economic benefit to the project. Tax-exempt bonds are available in most states and can offer 100% debt financing at long-term fixed rates.

Tax-exempt bonds, however, often require hurdling a number of restrictions, although they are less severe than those required to obtain federal loans or mortgage insurance. The process of obtaining bonds is lengthier than that for conventional financing, usually ranging from four to six months. Up-front financing fees are greater than those required for conventional loans as well. They include an investment banker's fee, a bond counsel fee, and printing costs. Under the new tax laws, tax-exempt bonds may be more difficult to obtain, requiring more qualifications and more paperwork.

To take advantage of tax-exempt bonds, many proprietary developers are able to obtain tax-exempt status. The bonds, also called industrial development bonds or IDBs, offer two options under Section 103(b) of the Internal Revenue Code for elderly housing firms: small-issue bonds and multifamily housing revenue bonds. Both are issued by a state or local agency, with the proceeds then loaned to the developer. The disadvantage of small-issue bonds is the capital expenditure ceiling of $10 million. Because of this, the small-issue bond market is dominated by nonprofit firms which, upon qualifying for a nonprofit exemption under Section 501(c)(3) of the Internal Revenue Code, are no longer subject to the dollar limitation.

Most development firms employ the multifamily residential bond, which has no restriction on capital expenditure. These bonds, however, require a developer to set aside 20% of a project's units to low- or moderate-income residents, defined as those families at or below 80% of the median household income for a family of four in the region. Because most elderly units are occupied by only one or two residents, this restriction is not as low as it seems. But the Treasury Department has recommended altering this restriction to reflect the income of a family of two rather than four persons. In the Phoenix area, for example, the rent for a low to moderate subsidized unit would fall from $534 to $350 under this recommendation.

Another restriction placed on the bonds requires a facility to remain rental for at least 10 years after it reaches 50% occupancy or one-half of the life of the bond issue, whichever is longer. Projects using multifamily housing revenue bonds must be "residential rental property," which has been interpreted to mean that units must have kitchens. Some of the requirements of meeting this definition are interpreted on a case-by-case basis.

The amount of interest paid by the developer will vary depending on the bond rating, which fluctuates with the assumed risk of the bond. To obtain a lower rating, most developers obtain credit enhancements such as a letter of credit or, more often, federal mortgage insurance from the Federal Housing Administration. Federal mortgage insurance, particularly that obtained under the 221(d)(4) program of the FHA, is provided to private lenders against mortgage losses for both conventionally financed projects and those financed through tax-exempt bonds. If the mortgage goes into default, FHA mortgage insurance pays an amount generally equaling 99% of the outstanding balance. Insurance is also available under Sections 221(d)(3) and 231 of the FHA, but is used less often because of lower lending limits.

Federal mortgage insurance contains a number of restrictions. Perhaps the most significant is a prohibition on charging an entry fee. This provision has effectively made the insurance unavailable to lifecare facilities and has encouraged the development of facilities that charge on a month-to-month or a fee-for-service basis. Other federal mortgage insurance restrictions prohibit medical services as a part of a project, without approval of the FHA's central office; allow no more than one meal each day provided through monthly fees;

prohibit the developer from applying to the federal low-income housing Section 8 program; and require the project to be set aside for elderly occupants only or for a fixed percentage of elderly. The processing time for FHA mortgage insurance is lengthy, averaging nine to 12 months.

Under the Davis-Bacon Act, all multifamily projects insured by the FHA must pay construction workers the prevailing wages for the region, as determined by the Department of Labor. Additionally, a six-month debt service reserve must be maintained for two years after project completion or occupancy. Fees required when filing for FHA insurance include an examination fee, an inspection fee, a mortgage insurance premium, and a financing/placement fee.

Nonprofit developers can make use of construction or rehabilitation loans provided by the Department of Housing and Urban Development. The program, offered under Section 202 of the HUD Act of 1959, provides 40-year loans for up to 100% of total development costs. The below-market rate is tied to the U.S. Treasury discount borrowing rate. The difficulties with this program include its low level of federal funding and, once again, the numerous restrictions placed on the project. The program requires that 10% of the units be accessible to the handicapped and 20% be set aside for Section 8 residents. Also, the sponsor of the project cannot be a nursing home, hospital, or religious group. A summary of HUD elderly housing program activities and their scope is illustrated in Table 6.2.

In Washington, New York, and other states that prohibit tax-exempt revenue bonds, nonprofit sponsors are often able to turn to taxable bonds, which can finance up to 100% of a project. However, these generally require a higher interest rate and offer shorter terms and amortization periods than tax-exempt bonds. As with conventional mortgages, the availability of the bonds is tied to market conditions and the developer's credit-worthiness. These bonds are viewed as risky and remain unrated by Moody's or Standard & Poor's. However, California has started to offer insurance for taxable bond issues, reducing their riskiness and lowering interest rates. A summary of the strengths of for-profit and not-for-profit operation and financing is listed below.

For-Profit (Market Rate Financing)

- Quicker funding decisions
- Fewer government requirements, quotas, or restrictions regarding resident population, rent level, operations, and physical plant
- Fewer costs of complying with government regulation
- Greater flexibility in lending terms, covenants, and financial arrangements
- Sources of funding less subject to variable and political government funding allocations

Not-for-Profit (Tax-Exempt and Subsidized Housing)

- Lower interest rate and annual debt service

- Greater credibility in marketing project to seniors
- Greater acceptance among conventional lenders with government mortgage insurance or letter of credit
- Possible reduced negative tax implications with prepaid income and imputed interest on endowment fees
- Longer loan amortization periods

Table 6.2. Summary of HUD Elderly Housing Program Activities[1]

Sections	Program	Status of Program	No. of Projects	Mortgages	Units	Elderly Units	% Elderly Units	Cum.
			Unassisted Programs					
231	Mortgage insurance of housing for elderly	Active	497	66,145	1,154,003,727	66,145	100.0	12/31/84
221(d)(3)	Multifamily rental	Active	3,611	364,733	6,064,514,303	26,373	7.2	
221(d)(4)	housing for low- and moderate-income families	Active	6,809	737,750	19,594,056,632	104,378	14.1	
207	Multifamily rental housing	Active	1,893	244,127	3,645,471,074	3,879	1.6	
232	Nursing home and intermediate care facilities	Active	1,488	178,558	2,491,653,517	178,558	100.0	
			Assisted Programs					
Title II	Low-income housing	Active	14,994	1,469,008	N/A	384,948		6/30/84
202	Direct loans for housing of elderly and handicapped	Active	2,537	180,752	6,081,449,912	154,865	85.7	
235[2]	Homeownership assistance for low- and moderate-income families	Inactive[3]	N/A	473,033	8,456,660,790	66,224	14.0	
		Active	N/A	117,089	4,409,450,088	3,981	3.4	
236	Rental and Co-op assistance for low- and moderate-income families	Inactive	4,058	435,891	7,577,614,685	56,128	12.9	
202/236	202/236 conversion	Inactive	182	28,591	487,075,452	28,591	100.0	
8[4]	Low income rental assistance:							
	Existing	Active	17,163	1,226,880	3,454,920,013	342,186	27.9	
	New construction	Active	8,339	534,536	2,717,369,316	299,192	56.0	
	Substantial rehab	Active	1,663	122,612	768,341,253	46,273	37.7	
23	Low Rent Leased Housing	Inactive	N/A	163,267	N/A	54,000+	35.0	6/85

[1] Figures obtained from Management Information Systems Division, Housing, Department of Housing and Urban Development, April 1985.

[2] 235 figures are based on CY 1982 recertifications.

[3] Figures on inactive line are for original program; figures on active line are for revised program.

[4] Excludes 202/8 reservations.

SOURCE: Judith Ann Hancock, ed., Housing the Elderly (Piscataway, N.J.: Center for Urban Policy Research of Rutgers University, 1987), p. 271.

Entry Fees

To build endowment-fee lifecare facilities, some developers are using a fee system to attract funding from future residents before the project gets off the ground. Relying on preconstruction sales requires the sponsor to apply future entrance fees to the capital debt, and, accordingly, the financial health of the facility becomes dependent on actuarial projections and resident turnover. Most sponsors cushion their financial security by establishing significant cash reserves.

A major issue involved in the use of entry fees is their effect on the sponsor's tax status. Entry fees may be income or capital, since the IRS has ruled that all money received is income unless intent clearly shows otherwise. Of course, this is not a problem for nonprofit sponsors. To avoid taxation, many sponsors are now offering partially or fully refundable entrance fees, normally set at a high rate. Under this option, the project can still be permanently funded by the fees; a departing resident is repaid when his or her vacated apartment is filled by a new resident paying a new entrance fee. Another option available to sponsors is the formation of a limited partnership or corporation to sell stock to residents of the project, thereby creating a cooperative. Cooperatives are becoming a more common financing technique.

Lending Practices: A Survey

The conventional financing arena for elderly housing is complex and fluctuating because of the relative newness of the industry and the lack of track records for many projects. Many lenders have shied away from the senior housing market because it represents a specialized property type with a limited demand market. For financial institutions entering this market, lending practices have yet to be standardized, varying greatly by type of facility, lender experience, and appraisal and feasibility study quality.

In an attempt to pinpoint typical lender policies and views, Arthur Gimmy International, prepared and distributed a questionnaire to 318 members of the Mortgage Bankers Association of America. The participants represented major lending institutions located in metropolitan areas throughout the United States. The response rate was 25%, an above-average return. The distribution of sample respondents is shown in Table 6.3.

Table 6.3.   Location of Survey Respondents

Region	Number of Respondents	Percent
West	26	33.3
Northeast	19	24.4
Midwest	16	20.5
Southwest	8	10.3
Southeast	6	7.7
National	3	3.8
Total	78	100.0

General Information

A full spectrum of lending institutions are involved in retirement housing. Included in the survey were mortgage bankers (39.4% of respondents), commercial banks (30.3%), savings and loan associations (15.8%), and insurance companies (9.2%). The remaining 5.3% of respondents fell into a miscellaneous category. The survey's typical lender was a medium-sized institution with less than $2.5 billion in assets (57.9% of respondents). Less than 10% had assets in excess of $25 billion.

Virtually all the lenders sampled are relatively inexperienced in this field. The typical respondent has made only six loans for all retirement facilities, including congregate facilities independent living facilities, CCRCs, board and care homes, and nursing homes. Table 6.4 gives an idea of the depth of experience among lenders.

Table 6.4.   Number of Loans per Lender

Number of Loans	Number of Respondents	Percent
1–5	21	47.7
6–10	12	27.3
11–24	6	13.6
Over 25	5	11.4
Total	44	100.0

Respondents were polled on what type of projects, and how many of each, they have financed in the past. Because recent times have seen new varieties of projects, the numbers do not reflect property types currently being built. Nursing homes led the list (29 responses with an average of 10 loans), followed by congregate facilities (26 responses with an average of 7.3 loans), independent living facilities (24 responses with an average of 6.2 loans), board and care homes (16 responses with an average of 2.4 loans), CCRCs (8 responses with an average of 2.1 loans), and CC (4 responses with an average of 7.0 loans).

Mortgage Terms

No consistency apparently exists among mortgage terms offered by the lenders for retirement projects. Loan-to-value ratios, interest rates, debt-coverage ratios, financing fees, and loan terms all vary greatly. One surprising finding is that, based on typical loan-to-value ratios, lenders did not differentiate between a loan based on the value determined as of the completion of a proposed project before occupancy begins (as is required to conform with current appraisal regulations), and the value of the project when it reaches a stabilized occupancy. Only 24% of the respondents state that the loan was based on the discounted value. A few respondents indicated that the discounted value for a nonstabilized project was the "floor" and the value at stabilized occupancy was the "ceiling" for determining the total loan amount.

The survey findings indicate that the loan-to-value ratios for projects are virtually the same as those for both good commercial investment properties and well located and designed apartment developments. The median loan-to-value ratio was 78%, while the range of loan-to-value ratios is listed in Table 6.5.

Table 6.5. Typical Loan-to-Value Ratios

Loan-to-Value Ratio	Number of Respondents	Percent
80% or more	12	27.3
75%–79%	15	34.1
70%–74%	10	22.7
65%–69%	4	9.1
60%–64%	2	4.5
Under 60%	1	2.3
Total	44	100.0

Interest rates offered on retirement projects were also comparable to those for typical investment properties. The median interest rate for a retirement project was 10.6% at the time of the survey (mid-1986). It is interesting to note that the cost of money does not seem to be that much different from capitalization rates used in the appraisal of retirement projects.

Table 6.6. Typical Interest Rate

Rate Range	Number of Respondents	Percent
9.0%– 9.9%	7	17.9
10.0%–10.9%	20	51.3
11.0%–11.9%	11	28.2
Over 12%	1	2.6
Total	39	100.0

Debt-coverage ratios, used by lenders to determine the size of a loan based on the cash flow produced by a project, are highly variable. We expected to find that typical debt-coverage ratios would be 1.25 or greater. However, there are as many responses below 1.25 as above, as shown in Table 6.7.

Table 6.7.   Typical Debt-Coverage Ratios

Debt-Coverage Ratios	Number of Respondents	Percent
1.0 –1.1	5	11.9
1.11–1.15	9	21.4
1.16–1.20	8	19.0
1.21–1.25	7	16.7
1.26–1.30	9	21.4
Over 1.30	4	9.5
Total	42	99.9

It may well be that debt-coverage ratios are influenced by property type. If this is the case, certain types of retirement projects such as nursing homes, which typically depend on government-funded Medicare and Medicaid programs for a large part of their income, could be perceived as having a lower degree of risk and may be pulling down the debt-coverage ratios. To some degree the above findings illustrate that lenders' inexperience in this field prevents them from measuring risk factors relative to projected future revenues appropriately.

Typical loan call periods offered by the surveyed lenders were also spread across the board. Excluding construction or bridge loans with very short terms of less than two years, the balance of respondents indicated that there were as many loans with terms of less than 15 years as those of more than 15 years. Twenty-seven percent of the respondents stated that the amortization period should not exceed 20 years. Again, this shows a tendency for lenders to view elderly projects as comparable to good quality standard apartment or commercial properties.

Financing charges such as fees or points were also highly variable, reflecting the inexperience of lenders in this field, varying perceptions of risk factors,

Table 6.8.   Typical Loan Call Terms

Loan Term (Years)	Number of Respondents	Percent
5 or less	12	29.3
6–9	7	17.1
10–15	10	24.4
16–20	1	2.4
20 or more	11	26.8
Total	41	100.0

availability of funds, and other loan underwriting considerations. The median financing charge was 2.0%; however, practices vary greatly, as shown in Table 6.9.

Table 6.9. Typical Financing Fees or Points

Fees/Points	Number of Respondents	Percent
Under 1.0%	4	9.5
1.0%–1.5%	11	26.2
1.6%–2.0%	7	16.7
2.1%–2.5%	12	28.6
2.6%–3.0%	4	9.5
Over 3.1%	4	9.5
Total	42	100.0

Appraisal Considerations

Respondents were asked how they felt appraisals of retirement projects could be improved. In order of importance, they suggested

1. Inclusion of a market analysis
2. Use of applicable retirement projects as comparables
3. Requiring experience in the field before accepting an assignment
4. Better investigation of the market's depth
5. Adequate support for income and expense projections
6. Consideration of future competitive projects
7. Requiring an independent feasibility study

Virtually all the lenders agreed that the first six items were roughly equal in importance. Lenders strongly supported including in the appraisals an in-depth market analysis or financial feasibility study prepared by a specialist in the field.

Most lenders involved in financing retirement projects, as compared with other types of real estate, require that the borrower contract with a professional management firm for the day-to-day operation of the business. Eighty-five percent of respondents stated that this was a requirement. This indicates that there will be on-going opportunities for specialists in this area as the number of retirement projects throughout the United States continues to grow in the next decade.

A key part of the market study for a proposed project is the calculation of market saturation rates, a financial technique used to measure overall market demand within a particular region. A market saturation rate describes the percentage of the qualifying population whose demand is or will be met by an existing or future product. This rate is part of a detailed demographic study of the primary and secondary markets, with age levels distributed on the basis of income brackets. Again, it appears that lender inexperience with retirement housing influences the level of acceptable market saturation rates. Those lenders specializing in retirement housing emphasize lower rates, while the others will allow a higher rate. An analyst should recognize, however, that saturation rate analysis should be adjusted to reflect the pricing, overall quality, and service package of the specific project.

About 30% of respondents indicated that a market saturation rate of 4% was the maximum they would allow on an approved project loan. Another 30% indicated that a market saturation rate between 5% and 9% was acceptable, while the balance of respondents (37.5%) found rates as high as 10% to 15% acceptable.

Market Trends

Participants were asked to give their opinions of trends taking place in the retirement housing field and the reasons why they were not making loans at this time. Of the lenders who had not entered the elderly market at the time of the survey, about 36% said they expected to be involved in the financing of retirement projects in the future. The responses of those who stated that they were not going to make retirement loans are summarized in Table 6.10.

Table 6.10. Reasons for Not Making Retirement Housing Loans

	Number of Respondents	Percent
Too special-purpose design	9	26.5
Too management-intensive	7	20.6
Questionable financial feasibility	6	17.7
Too many inexperienced operators and developers	6	17.7
Market too difficult to quantify	4	11.7
Market will be overbuilt in near future	2	5.8
Total	34	100.0

Lenders generally pinpointed two critical factors to explain their conservatism. Many lenders explained their wariness of projects that require specialized management and have a limited-purpose design that is not suitable for alternative uses. Others said they expect that the market will be overbuilt in the future because of the great amount of developer attention retirement housing is now receiving. Responses such as these suggest a continuing lender uncertainty about the retirement housing market. To overcome this caution, developers should undertake considerable market research for any future proposal, engage the services of a professional management firm with a good track record, and hire consultants with extensive experience in elderly housing.

7

Market and Financial Feasibility Studies

In Chapter Two, we examined the major demographic trends spurring developer interest in senior housing. But this growing market is not enough to ensure a successful project. Because the elderly population is heterogeneous and the senior housing industry is untested, developers should acquire a detailed knowledge of specific markets. The first step in this direction is the preparation of a detailed, focused market and financial feasibility study.

A market study surveys the subject's competitive environment, while a financial study quantifies these competitive influences into financial projections. The two studies are complementary and the conclusions reached in each must be consistent and supported by the market.

The goal of a market analysis is to define and demonstrate whether a specific market exists in sufficient size to allow a proposed project to achieve profitability within a reasonable period of time. A market study can also be used to ascertain whether a sufficient market exists to support an existing project in the foreseeable future.

A financial feasibility study analyzes a proposed or existing project's economic viability in the short, medium, and long term. Annual cash flows are forecast and used to measure overall project profitability and the required yield on investment.

This chapter will provide definitions and a framework for preparing detailed market and financial feasibility studies, which are prerequisites to the effective evaluation and appraisal of any existing or proposed elderly housing project.

Market Analysis

A market feasibility study or market analysis is an in-depth examination of the regional supply and demand factors shaping the viability of a specific project. A well-prepared study will follow the outline shown in Figure 7.1.

Figure 7.1. Outline of a Market Feasibility Study

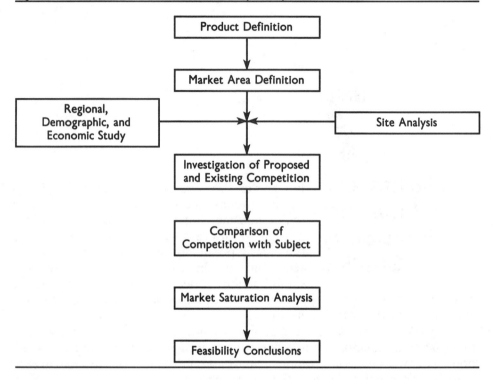

The study should be prepared by an appraiser or an independent real estate market research firm. While a market feasibility study prepared by a developer is likely to include relevant data, it can lack objectivity and is not acceptable to a lender. A detailed market analysis is a requirement in every well documented appraisal. A limited number of research firms are capable of producing detailed, unbiased market feasibility studies. However, in-depth studies are likely to be quite costly and time-consuming.

A thoroughly prepared market study serves many purposes. First, it provides a clear understanding of the project to be built and the market to be served. Second, the decisions of lenders are greatly influenced by a well-supported and documented report. Third, detailed market analysis forces the developer to consider the project in relation to its competitive environment. This will aid in the creation of a marketing campaign prior to opening and also helps determine rent or fee levels, a service package, the unit layout, and the unit mix. Finally, the market feasibility study generates evidence needed to prepare a financial feasibility study, which the appraiser uses to convert the estimated cash flow into value.

Project Definition

The consultant or appraiser begins the market feasibility study by consulting with the developer and identifying which specific type of elderly project is being examined. This step defines the competition and establishes the parameters for the financial feasibility study that will follow. Each major elderly housing type—skilled nursing, personal care, continuing care, low- and high-end congregate housing, and retirement communities—has unique types of revenue sources, incurs different categories of expenses, and exists in separate competitive environments. For these reasons, defining the specific housing type is a critical step.

Though a market feasibility study is usually tailored to one type of facility, a more open-ended and comprehensive market study can be undertaken early in the development process before the developer has settled on a single type of facility. This broader market analysis helps the developer evaluate the most feasible housing alternative by examining the risks, pitfalls, and potential returns of various types of housing, employing different levels of health care and services. Once this preliminary market analysis is complete, a more detailed market and financial feasibility study is then needed to evaluate the alternative chosen.

Market Area Definition

In our experience, most forms of elderly housing have a primary target market area extending to a maximum of about 10 to 15 miles from the site, except in rural areas. As mentioned earlier, this area is small because the elderly have a strong tendency to stay within their immediate community when first choosing to live in a senior development and prefer to remain a reasonable driving distance from relatives and friends. However, a project is likely to have a smaller target market area in more densely populated areas because of greater competition; primary market areas can be as small as five miles around the site. Conversely, the more unique a facility or the more aggressive its marketing campaign, the greater likelihood that it will attract residents from outside a traditional primary market area. For example, large-scale resort retirement communities are likely to draw residents from greater distances, including many from out of state.

Perhaps more important than a definition of market area based strictly on distance, is the overall character of the project's environment, whether it be urban, suburban, small town, or rural. With most forms of elderly housing, however, approximately 80% of total estimated demand for a facility will be drawn from the primary market area. This is supported by data accumulated by Laventhol & Horwath that is summarized in Table 7.1.

Table 7.1. Primary Market Area and Proximity to Children

	Principally Retirement Center	Oriented Toward Nursing Care
Percentage of communities which estimate their primary market area to be:		
5 to 10 mile radius	24%	24%
11 to 15 mile radius	21%	6%
16 to 20 mile radius	13%	6%
21 to 25 mile radius	22%	37%
Over 25 mile radius	20%	27%
Percentage of residents estimated to come from within their primary market area:		
Lower quartile	60%	75%
Median	80%	80%
Upper quartile	90%	90%
Percentage of residents who have children estimated to live within 30 minutes driving time[1]		
Urban communities	45%	50%
Suburban or rural communities	55%	62%

[1] Amounts are medians.
SOURCE: Laventhol & Horwath, *Lifecare Retirement Center Industry, 1985*, p. 16. Reprinted with permission.

The remaining 20% will be drawn from the facility's secondary market area, the boundaries of which can vary greatly. These boundaries are determined primarily by the region's population density and any competitive senior developments. In general, the primary market area for urban facilities is from 5 to 10 miles, for suburban facilities 5 to 20 miles, and for small town and rural facilities 20 to 30 miles.

Site Analysis

In Chapter Four, we discussed those characteristics important in the evaluation of a site for elderly housing. Among these are traditional evaluation criteria such as the site's zoning, shape and topography, access, availability of improvements, and the quality of the surrounding neighborhood. Something equally important is the site's proximity to essential support services, which are critical in elderly housing because of many seniors' reduced mobility. These support services include medical facilities such as acute care hospitals, clinics, and skilled nursing facilities; religious institutions; retail stores and banks; and recreational centers such as parks, golf courses, and senior centers.

Analysis of alternative sites is typically conducted early in the development process, usually by the developer without the assistance of outside consultants. When comparing the subject to other properties, key factors to examine include cost, terms of purchase, and proximity to competition. Many developers acquire options to purchase a specific site. These allow the developer to evaluate a site comprehensively and obtain any government approvals before making a large financial commitment to the site.

Investigation of Existing and Proposed Competition

Investigating both existing and proposed competition is probably the most important part of a market feasibility study. A project's potential profitability is obviously linked to its competitive environment. Because of the specialized, shallow elderly housing market, it is vital for the appraiser or consultant to identify all competing facilities. A thorough analysis of the competition not only helps determine if a specific market is overbuilt, but also allows a developer to tailor the project in a unique way to create or satisfy untapped market preferences.

Identifying the subjects' housing type and defining its target market area sets the parameters for searching out competitive facilities. Because other facilities are unlikely to be identical to the subject, the appraiser should define "competitive" loosely. A lack of existing competition should not automatically be construed to mean that a particular market area is ripe for elderly housing. It may mean instead that demand is weak or city approval is difficult to obtain. It can also portend the necessity of a more intensive marketing campaign to educate the market area about elderly housing.

The best direct market evidence for forecasting the prospects of the subject is existing competitive projects. Proposed competitive projects, though influencing market acceptance of the subject, have yet to be tested for market acceptance themselves. Existing facilities can be identified from sources such as

- The yellow pages
- City, county, and state housing authorities
- Local planning departments
- The local chamber of commerce
- National indexes including *The National Continuing Care Directory* and *The National Directory of Retirement Facilities*[1]
- Other competitive facilities
- Local senior organizations

Once identified, the appraiser should visit each facility. A checklist of data to gather during a tour of projects is provided in Table 7.2.

---

[1] *The National Continuing Care Directory* (Washington, D.C.: American Association of Retired Persons, 1984) and *The National Directory of Retirement Facilities* (Phoenix, AZ: Onyx Press, 1986).

Table 7.2. Comparable Facility Site Visit Checklist

Name _____

Location _____

Miles from subject _____

Age of facility _____

Total number of units _____

Site Data

Quality of surrounding neighborhood _____

Proximity to major services

    Medical _____

    Religious _____

    Retail _____

    Recreation _____

Project Construction Data

Construction and landscaping
  quality _____

Overall project impression _____

	Studios	1 Bedroom	2 Bedrooms	3 Bedrooms
Unit mix	_____	_____	_____	_____
Unit sizes	_____	_____	_____	_____
Monthly rental/fee	_____	_____	_____	_____
Double occupancy	_____	_____	_____	_____
Additional fees	_____	_____	_____	_____
Unit availability	_____	_____	_____	_____
Occupancy rates	_____	_____	_____	_____

Services

Health care offered on site _____

Amenities package

    Number of meals _____

    Frequency of housekeeping _____

    Social services _____

    Transportation _____

The appraiser's next step is the identification of the proposed competition. These projects can greatly affect the market acceptance and the ultimate success or failure of the subject. In active markets, the number of proposed competitive facilities can change very quickly. Markets can become overbuilt in a matter of months if a large number of competitive facilities commit to a region at the same time. Though data involving proposed facilities are sometimes difficult to gather, an appraiser should search diligently. Among the best sources for information are city planning officials and building department files, the client developer, and the competing developers or owners themselves.

The appraiser should assess the status of the proposed projects, the scheduled date of occupancy, and the probability of final construction. These may be difficult to evaluate because financing uncertainties can delay or sometimes kill a project. Because objective information is difficult to acquire, an analyst would be wise to recognize a worst-case scenario where most or all of the feasible, proposed, competitive projects are eventually built.

Comparison of Subject to Competition

Conducting a market analysis of competitive properties is most productive when the properties are compared directly with the subject. Key comparative data include the fee or monthly rent per square foot, unit mix, amenities package, and age and quality of the subject. Characteristics of the subject and competitive facilities can be arrayed by a range (highest to lowest), average or mean, and most comparable basis. Ratings on a scale of one to five can be used to arrive at a quantitative evaluation of the competition with regard to location characteristics (such as access and proximity to recreation, health, retail, and cultural facilities) and building quality aspects (such as project construction and design, amenities, unit layout, and unit size).

These comparisons will help place the subject in its competitive environment. The goal of comparing the subject to other projects is to identify an overcrowded or unfilled market and to estimate selling prices, a market rent, or a fee structure for the subject.

Market Saturation Analysis

Market saturation analysis is a method of estimating overall market saturation of elderly housing units within a market area, or the degree to which a market is overbuilt or is fertile for elderly housing. This calculation assists the sponsor, lender, appraiser, and consultant in estimating the project's feasibility, its market rent or fee, and its absorption rate and pattern. Market saturation analysis involves the following steps.

1. Measuring the theoretical size of the subject's target market
2. Determining the total number of competitive units
3. Calculating the total market saturation rate required to fill all proposed and existing comparable facilities, both with and without the subject
4. Analyzing the overall feasibility of the subject given the calculated market saturation rates

Market saturation analysis begins by determining the size of the target market. The target market is defined as the number of age- and income-qualifying elderly households within a certain region, which is determined in an earlier phase of the feasibility study. The number of age- and income-qualifying elderly households can be taken directly or extrapolated from U.S. census data. Though local government agencies and chambers of commerce are good sources of census data, nationwide demographic service firms such as National Planning Data Corporation, National Decision Systems, Public

Demographics, Inc., and CACI offer census data in formats that are tailored for business and easily used. More importantly, they will provide (for a fee) data more recent than the 1980 census by extrapolating the census to population estimates for the current year and projections for future years.

Three variables are used to construct different scenarios in calculating the market saturation rates. The first variable is market area. This can be defined by existing political boundaries or geographic lines around a site.

Second, the age of the new tenants is considered. Minimum age for entrants is usually set at 65, 70, or 75. Using 65 years of age is an aggressively optimistic scenario, since the average age of residents entering retirement centers ranges from the lower to upper 70s.

The third variable among the target market is annual income. Minimum incomes usually range from $15,000 to $25,000 and up, depending on the financial requirements and the planned rent or fee of the facility. Determining the minimum income level necessary to meet monthly rent or service payments is difficult and subject to different interpretations. Many analysts believe that a senior can afford to spend a maximum of 80% of his or her income on the rent or fee of a senior project. One consultant's estimates are shown in Table 7.3 in the form of an affordability chart. These estimates do not incorporate asset bases—home equity, pension funds, relatives—that can be drawn on to meet monthly rents and fees.

Table 7.3. Affordability of Rental Retirement Housing

Households that can afford monthly payment[1] of more than:

	$800	$1000	$1200	$1500	$1800	$2200
One-person households						
65–69	1,062,000	794,000	573,000	428,000	222,000	176,000
70–74	905,000	518,000	391,000	197,000	128,000	107,000
75 and over	1,446,000	885,000	556,000	390,000	340,000	320,000
Subtotal	3,413,000	2,197,000	1,520,000	1,015,000	690,000	603,000
Two-person households						
65–69	2,272,000	1,797,000	1,240,000	876,000	611,000	513,000
70–74	1,569,000	1,249,000	914,000	484,000	320,000	171,000
75 and over	1,943,000	1,678,000	1,177,000	737,000	725,000	570,000
Subtotal	5,784,000	4,724,000	3,331,000	2,097,000	1,656,000	1,254,000
Total 65 and over	9,197,000	6,921,000	4,851,000	3,112,000	2,346,000	1,857,000
Households that can afford payments as percentage of total households (by age group)						
65 and over	51%	38%	27%	17%	13%	10%
70 and over	48%	35%	25%	15%	12%	9%
75 and over	46%	35%	24%	15%	15%	12%

[1] Including one meal per day, utilities, linen service, transportation, housekeeping, etc. Proceeds from home equity assumed to be invested at 10%.

SOURCE: Real Estate Research Corporation, Rental Retirement Housing: New Opportunities (Chicago: 1986).

Different combinations of these three variables can be used in calculating saturation rates. A common method is to create a combination that reflects a pessimistic, most likely, and optimistic forecast, as illustrated in Table 7.4.

Table 7.4. Market Saturation Analysis, Number of Qualifying Households

Year: XXXX

Parameters	Pessimistic	Scenarios[1] Most Likely	Optimistic
Market area	5 mile ring	10 mile ring	20 mile ring
Age	80+	75+	70+
Income	$25,000+	$20,000+	$15,000+
Number of qualifying households	XXX	XXX	XXX

[1] Scenarios are illustrations only and do not represent average or typical scenarios.

After the target market has been defined, the appraiser determines the total number of competitive units. This total should include both existing and proposed comparable developments, and can be calculated in pessimistic, most likely, and optimistic scenarios. It is common to estimate the total number of competitive units in a market (for example, the total high-end congregate units within a 10-mile radius) both with and without the subject units. In this way, the difference represents the market penetration rate for the subject units only. The combinations of variables used to calculate market saturation are almost infinite. Any scenario should be reasonable, relevant, and meaningful.

The third step is a calculation of the market saturation rate required to fill all proposed and existing comparable facilities, again with and without the subject. The formula for this is

$$\text{Market Saturation Rate} = \frac{\text{Total Existing \& Proposed Competitive Units (with and without subject)}}{\text{Total Age- and Income-Qualifying Elderly Households}}$$

A calculated market saturation rate of, say, 8.3% would mean that about one out of twelve age- and income-qualifying seniors within a defined market area must choose to live in elderly housing to fill all existing or proposed competitive units within that market area.

The fourth and last step is to analyze the overall feasibility of the subject, given the calculated market saturation rates. Our experience, coupled with an extensive survey of lenders, supports the following guidelines for interpreting market saturation rates:

Calculated Saturation Level	Estimate of Overall Market Demand
Less than 5%	Conservative
5-10%	Moderate
10-15%	Aggressive
More than 15%	Speculative

According to these guidelines, a saturation level of 15% or less would show a potentially adequate level of market demand for the absorption of the region's elderly housing units, including the subject. A level higher than 15% can mean that a market is overbuilt. The calculated saturation levels are used to gauge the overall feasibility of the project and provide evidence for an estimate of the market rent or fee and absorption pattern and length. All other factors being roughly equal, a project will probably have shorter absorption periods with lower saturation rates and, conversely, will likely face longer absorption periods with higher saturation rates.

It is important to note what saturation analysis can and cannot do. Although this financial tool is useful in estimating overall market saturation, it does not address any existing or potential advantages or deficiencies that a specific project may offer. A particular saturation rate is not a guarantee of success or failure. A project's future is greatly influenced by its quality and location, the effectiveness of its marketing campaign, and other factors. Furthermore, market saturation rates can become meaningless if an appraiser improperly establishes the information on market area, age, income, and competitive units used to calculate the rate.

An example of market saturation analysis is illustrated later in this book in Chapter Ten.

Primary Market Research

Market saturation analysis is a method of measuring market demand using secondary (U.S. census) data. But an increasingly common method of estimating demand for a major project is the use of primary market research, including surveys, questionnaires, personal interviews, and focus study groups. (Surveying the competition is also a form of primary market research.) These studies, though often costly and time-consuming to conduct, can indicate demand and, in addition, act as a form of marketing for the project. Because of the time and cost involved, these studies are usually conducted only for sophisticated, high-end congregate projects and CCRCs.

In survey research, a consultant samples the target population through mailed questionnaires, telephone interviews, or one-on-one interviews. Of these methods, questionnaires often produce the highest response rate because of their anonymity. They are also relatively less cumbersome to conduct and tabulate. The main objective of survey research is to identify potential residents and help design the future marketing campaign. Surveys typically request information such as

- Where the senior currently lives and for how long
- The senior's interest in elderly housing
- The senior's reasons for moving
- The unit sizes and services preferred
- The level of on-site medical services desired
- How much the senior would be willing or able to pay

Focus study research, as discussed in Chapter Four, involves comprehensive questioning of a small group of elderly persons, usually in groups of five to 20. The purpose of the focus study is to test the acceptance of the subject, its unit layout, and its service package. Focus study groups can also generate word-of-mouth advertising for a development. Typical areas of focus group discussion include project design, unit design and size, site location, services, awareness of competition, and the entry fee/rental option. The sessions, usually lasting a few hours, are open-ended and nonjudgmental; of course, there are no "correct" opinions. It is also important to remember that they are designed to gather information and should not be used as a forum for high-pressure selling.

Rent/Entry Fee and Absorption Period Estimates

It is important to keep in mind the ultimate objectives of a market study, namely, a judgment about the overall competitive atmosphere of a project, an estimate of market rents or fees, and a forecast of absorption patterns. These conclusions are helpful later in the preparation of the financial feasibility study. The market study also provides market evidence for estimating the percentage of units that will be preleased or presold before initial occupancy.

There are few universal guidelines for estimating rents or entry fees. Depending on location and competition, these can range from $500 to $2,500 per month for rental projects and $15,000 to $500,000 for endowment projects. Average rents can be double or triple the standard apartment rents within any market. Factors to consider in estimating rents or fees include the rent levels of the most comparable facilities (existing comparables should be given more weight than those proposed), characteristics of the subject in relation to the competition, developer estimates, market saturation rates, and the depth and breadth of the marketing campaign.

For the absorption period, the industry standard for average-sized, proposed senior projects has traditionally been 18 to 24 months. However, with increasing competition in the industry, absorption period estimates of 24 to 48 months are not uncommon. In general, senior projects lease up slower than standard housing because of the residents' larger financial commitment. An exception is elderly projects that are government subsidized or supported. Because these projects are attractive, offering near-equal services for lower rents, they usually experience rapid lease-up periods of 12 months or less.

Forecasting an absorption rate of 10 or more units per month is considered aggressive; six to seven units per month is a more common and realistic estimate. These guidelines do not take into account the possibility of a project's unique characteristics or particular marketing campaign. Extra care must be taken when using comparable facilities that have experienced quicker lease-up periods. These facilities are often the first or second facility in a market, which generally translates into a fast absorption of units. Lenders in particular favor a conservative estimate of the lease-up pattern.

In addition to the factors listed above, absorption period analysis requires an estimate of the extent of preleasing. Common estimates of preleasing percentages range from 10% to 25%. These estimates are highly dependent on market saturation rates, rent levels, and the intensity of the marketing campaign. Financial commitments and letters of intent prior to the opening are tangible sources for estimating the extent of preleasing. Some states and lenders also require tangible evidence of high levels (up to 50%) of financial commitment in the form of deposits before approving commencement of construction for some types of elderly housing such as CCRCs.

Financial Feasibility

With a financial feasibility study, the appraiser forecasts the financial data needed for estimating a project's yearly cash flows and the overall return on investment. A financial or economic feasibility study measures the financial viability of a project through income and expense projections based on information contained in the market feasibility study. Though financial forecasting is an imprecise science, the most reliable forecasts are based on direct market evidence. As the elderly housing industry matures, lending institutions will require financial estimates that are well documented and supported by the market, instead of by general knowledge obtained through "experience." This is especially true for elderly housing development, in which every project is unique in some way.

The financial feasibility study begins with a well-prepared market feasibility study, which has already estimated market rents or fees. A financial feasibility study should follow the steps shown in Figure 7.2. Like a market feasibility study, a financial feasibility study can be prepared by a developer, owner, appraiser, or outside consultant. However, interpreting return on investment and estimating after-debt-service cash flow is a developer's responsibility and is usually beyond the scope of most appraisal and consulting assignments. A financial feasibility study serves the following purposes:

1. It helps fulfill lender requirements for assessing risk in meeting debt service payments;
2. It allows the developer to evaluate the overall riskiness and return on investment of a development;
3. It sets parameters and requirements for both interim and permanent financing levels;
4. It produces the annual budget estimates needed for proper short- and long-term cash management.

Figure 7.2. Outline of a Financial Feasibility Study

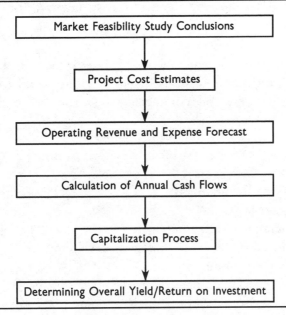

Project Cost Estimating

Evaluating financial feasibility begins with a projection of the total financial commitment involved in a project's construction. Project cost estimates are needed for forecasting seed money levels, determining interim and permanent financing levels, and evaluating funding options.

Development costs include the costs of raw land, land development, hard construction, landscaping, equipment and fixtures, all consulting fees and permits, interest reserves, lease-up reserves, marketing prior to the opening, and a contingency fund. Sources of information for the estimates include comparable projects, experienced architects and contractors, and the developer or appraiser's own prior development experience. Because costs vary greatly from region to region, the developer should strive to obtain specific cost bid estimates wherever practical. Actual bids and estimates can be a good source for determining financing costs; site development costs; consultant, architect, and engineering fees; and city permit and approval fees. Cost estimates should be as detailed as possible and should reflect time adjustments to the actual, estimated date of construction. Finally, the developer can calculate project costs not only on a total-dollar basis but also line by line on a per-unit and per-square-foot basis.

Project cost estimating should reflect the specialized nature of elderly housing. This includes the generally higher costs incurred for

- Cost of common facilities, including dining areas, medical care, and recreational space
- Specific construction requirements of state or local agencies
- Licensing, particularly for those projects with on-site medical care
- Additional interest and contingency fees for the extended lease-up period
- Higher marketing costs (up to $3,000 per unit)
- Greater expenditures for specially designed furniture and equipment
- Higher landscaping costs
- Lower parking requirements
- Larger storage areas
- Greater soundproofing requirements
- Inclusion of elevators in all multistory developments
- Central communication systems
- Inclusion of specially designed handicapped units
- Additional security features such as gates, security cameras, and monitors

Operating Revenues and Expenses

Property yields, annual cash flow requirements, and the estimated value of an income-producing property are all derived from an analysis of the property's annual cash flow generated from operations. Net annual cash flow from operations is simply the difference between all operating revenues and all operating expenses. This pro forma analysis should estimate operating revenues, costs, and escalations for a minimum three- to five-year period, with five years being the most common projection period. The appraiser should pay particular attention to forecasting operating revenues and expenses during the absorption period, because this period holds the highest risk for a lender. Reflecting this higher risk, absorption period pro forma income statements are usually broken into quarterly or monthly period increments. Once a property reaches a stabilized or full occupancy, annual period increments are sufficient.

Below is an example of the minimum information that should be reported in a cash flow or income statement for congregate rental elderly housing.

Revenues	Source of Data
Estimated gross rents collected	Market feasibility study
Double occupancy surcharges	
Miscellaneous income	

Expenses	Source of Data
Real estate taxes	Comparable developments, experienced senior housing managers
Insurance	
Maintenance	
General & administrative	
Activities	
Marketing	
Utilities	
Housekeeping	
Transportation	
Food service	

Buy-in congregate developments such as condominiums and cooperatives require an estimate of cash flows only during the absorption period, since future buyers or owners will be responsible for and will "own" annual cash flows. Expenses during the absorption period would include all operating expenses that the developer would incur on unsold spaces and selling costs.

CCRCs and lifecare facilities are the most complex form of elderly housing to analyze, because of on-site health care and buy-in endowments or membership fees, some of which are refundable. The analysis of buy-in fees in a cash flow estimate is influenced by state or local regulations, the refundability of the buy-in fee, and actuarial calculations used to estimate rent turnover. In addition to the revenues and expenses illustrated for congregate rental facilities, CCRCs have the additional cash flow components shown below.

Revenues	Source of Data
Endowment fees	Market feasibility study
Endowment appreciation income	Actuarial estimates
Reserve fund investment income	State regulations
Resident health care income	Local real estate trends
Nonmember health care income	
Health care insurance reimbursements	
Resale income	
Fee-for-service income	

Expenses	Source of Data
Endowment refunds and withdrawals	Comparable developments
Health care expenses	Actuarial estimates
Health care insurance	Experienced CCRC operators
Reserve fund	
Resale expenses	

CCRC annual cash flow projections can extend to 20 years, with 10 to 15 years being the most common. To set a projection period, the appraiser should look at actuarial data. The key factor is the date at which the facility will become actuarially stabilized or have a constant rate of unit turnover.

While detailed expense data from comparable facilities are often difficult to obtain, experienced managers of elderly housing are the best source. Fixed expenses, such as real estate taxes and insurance, can be gathered from direct quotes and bids. Variable expenses—those dependent on resident population—can be derived by line-by-line budgeting, on a per unit or per resident basis, or from a percentage of the effective gross income. Our experience in the appraisal of numerous elderly housing projects supports the following broad ranges for operating expenses as a percentage of effective gross revenue.

Standard multifamily housing	25%–35%
Congregate elderly (independent living)	40%–55%
Residential care	50%–70%
Skilled nursing care	70%–85%

These general rules of thumb should not replace a line-by-line estimate and analysis of expenses. Differences in operating expense percentages are dependent on the size of the project, due to economies of scale; average revenue per resident or patient; the degree of specialized management; project location; and the intensity of living or health care assistance given to residents or patients. The expense guidelines shown above reflect the basic differences in elderly housing types; for example, the intensity of living assistance and health care are greatest at a skilled nursing facility, which leads to higher expenses as a percentage of effective gross income.

Operating expenses as a percentage of effective gross income will obviously be higher during the absorption period. This reflects a combination of fixed expenses and a lower revenue base, as well as the operating inefficiencies and the lack of economies of scale existing at the time of a project's opening.

Ratio Analysis

Ratio analysis incorporates debt service cash flows into the analysis of net operating cash flows to arrive at the information needed for calculating a development's overall yield rates. The most common ratio to measure overall profitability is the return on investment ratio.

$$\text{(Annual Cash Flow from Operations)} - \text{(Annual Debt Service)} = \frac{\text{Net Cash Flow}}{\text{Total Equity}}$$

This ratio, also known as cash on cash return, can be calculated annually, on a net present value basis, or averaged over the projection period. The calculated return can then be evaluated by the developer according to his or her own risk and return criteria and comparisons to competing investments. Other common yield ratios include

- Annual net income/total development cost
- Profit (appraisal value less total development cost)/total development cost
- Annual after tax cash flow/total development cost
- Profit/equity
- Annual after tax cash flow/equity

To evaluate profitability, the developer or sponsor can employ other commonly used financial evaluation techniques, such as net present value analysis (discounted cash flow less total development cost), payback period analysis, and utility/probability analysis. Finally, each of the above techniques for quantifying a project's profitability can incorporate the tax effect of cash flows to each equity participant or to joint venture or syndication equity distributions, as appropriate.

8

The Appraisal Process: Influences On Value

The appraisal of elderly housing requires the use of conventional appraisal principles, methods, and techniques. However, elderly housing is a special-purpose property type, because of its on-site services and design requirements. As such, an appraiser should incorporate those unique factors into the valuation of both existing and proposed projects.

Elderly housing can be viewed as a combination of a residential project, whether it be rental, condominium, or cooperative in form; a hotel offering meals, housekeeping, and transportation; a social club offering activities; and a medical facility offering everything from personal living assistance to intensive, around-the-clock medical care. Using only one of these types of facilities in analyzing comparable market properties is not appropriate in most circumstances because it may fail to address the special orientation toward the elderly and the grouping of all these services at one site. The following discussion of the appraisal process focuses on these traits specific to elderly housing.

Elderly housing can be appraised by the three traditional approaches to value: the cost approach, the income capitalization approach, and the sales comparison approach. In most cases, the purpose of the appraisal is an estimate of market value derived from a reconciliation of the three approaches. As with many sophisticated property types, appraising elderly housing includes the development's going concern or business value. Consequently, a senior project's worth is more than just the value of the real estate assets; it also includes furniture and equipment, licenses, and the reputation or goodwill established by the business in the community. Therefore, in a reconciliation of the three approaches, the income capitalization approach, which incorporates business value, is usually given greatest weight. All of these realty and nonrealty components are reflected in the revenues produced by a project, but they are difficult to segregate individually using the cost or sales comparison approach. To comply with current appraisal standards, nonrealty components of value must be separately identified. This can be done by comparing the value estimates derived using the cost approach with those derived from the income capitalization and sales comparison approaches. In addition to an estimate of value for physical real estate depreciated (replacement cost new), a properly prepared appraisal using the cost approach will delineate nonrealty components of value such as furniture and equipment, business or going concern value, goodwill, and licenses, if applicable.

This chapter is the first of two detailing the appraisal process for elderly developments. In this chapter, we will discuss those descriptive factors that influence an appraiser's judgment when estimating a senior project's market value. Chapter 9 will focus on the cost, income capitalization, and sales comparison approaches to estimating market value.

Influences on Value

Regional and City Analysis

The regional description section of the appraisal contains a discussion of geography, political boundaries, population, demographics, housing, employment, economic development, transportation, climate, and cultural data. This information is important in assessing the overall development climate, measuring the cost of living, projecting potential demand, and defining the market area for a specific senior project. Special consideration should be given to demographic trends and projections for those 65 and over, existing geographic concentrations of elderly population, the extent of existing and proposed alternative housing for seniors, and the overall image as a community appropriate for a senior development. This specific information may be obtained at a community's chamber of commerce or economic development department. Many cities have recognized seniors as a distinct group of residents with special characteristics and needs and have developed extra services for them. For example, a chamber of commerce or housing authority may publish lists of privately available housing targeted to seniors. Another good source of data is local senior citizen organizations that direct seniors to housing opportunities and specialized services. Finally, demographic service companies can provide specific age, population, and income statistics for any defined area.

Neighborhood Analysis

This type of analysis involves a review of existing and proposed development within the immediate area of the subject site. An appraiser can garner information on neighborhood development trends through personal inspection and by talking with city officials, developers, and brokers familiar with an area. In analyzing a neighborhood, the appraiser should specifically determine

- Proximity to major medical (hospital, clinics, skilled nursing care), retail (banks, shopping, restaurants), religious, and recreational (movies, parks, golf courses) facilities
- Availability of public transportation

- Access from major thoroughfares and highways
- Overall neighborhood quality, including the nature and condition of surrounding development, affluence, rent levels, security, and reputation

After assessing the strengths and weaknesses of a specific site, the appraiser should draw a conclusion about the desirability of the location for elderly housing, including a discussion of potential external obsolescence.

Site Description

The site description section of an appraisal analysis deals with facts about the site's physical characteristics; existing improvements; access and exposure; assessments and taxes; easements and encumbrances; excess land; and zoning. Zoning information relevant to elderly housing would include a discussion of allowable higher densities, such as units per acre, and lower parking ratio requirements, or total parking spaces per total units. The appraiser should consider particular community requirements regarding design, construction detail, and landscaping. Because of the unique nature of elderly housing, most jurisdictions require a special design or environmental review. This could include a review of new traffic patterns created around a project or, more generally, the project's impact on its neighbors. If the project contains on-site medical care, the appraiser should consider possible state regulations regarding site preparation and development. Site information can be obtained through personal inspection, a review of the project's public file at city hall, and discussions with government officials, including assessors.

Description of Improvements

In the improvement description section, the appraiser should examine all building and improvement details relevant to the subject. These can be obtained from plans or drawings, discussions with the owner and project architect, and a review of the project's public file at city hall. The section should include a detailed discussion of unit mix, size, and design as specialized for elderly use. A description of unit design should specifically comment on soundproofing features, a central communication system, extent of unit kitchen and laundry facilities, features of handicapped units, and size of storage spaces.

By definition, a senior housing development will include a commons area where the residents are served meals and have access to recreational facilities. The discussion of the commons areas should include the dining room and kitchen, specialized recreational spaces, administrative offices, and distance and access from the residential units to the commons area.

In addition to a traditional discussion of landscaping detail, the appraiser should also identify any seating areas; additional security features, such as gates or perimeter walls; exterior recreation areas, such as a pool or shuffleboard court; residential gardening areas; and any above-average landscaping detail.

Finally, the appraiser should discuss whether the construction, detail, unit design, unit mix, and landscaping plan are appropriate for elderly housing. This includes identifying any physical inadequacies and functional inutilities by assessing the strengths and weaknesses of the subject's physical design relative to competitive projects. One technique for doing this is to use building area comparisons.

Market Analysis

The market analysis section of the appraisal analyzes the project's market feasibility. This section can also provide information about the industry by identifying the major types of elderly housing and their characteristics, while placing the subject in this industry context. The market feasibility analysis not only provides data for estimating market rents and absorption, which are used in the income capitalization approach, but is instrumental in determining the highest and best use of the site, which is needed for all three approaches to value. Therefore, though a study of competitive facilities is traditionally placed in the appraisal's income capitalization approach section, it should be dealt with separately.

To prepare a market feasibility report, a sponsor of a proposed project will sometimes retain an outside consultant, often a research firm or a real estate consultant specializing in elderly housing. Many lenders will require this type of third-party analysis for more sophisticated senior projects. A prudent developer will also understand the wisdom of obtaining an independent expert's opinion of a project.

The market feasibility study is usually prepared before the appraiser is retained and is therefore available for his or her use. While a well prepared market study can save an appraiser research time, it is still the appraiser's responsibility to assess independently any conclusions or opinions set forth in the study. This assessment should include an analysis of the consultant's research methods and a verification of comparable facility data. In the previous chapter, we discussed in detail the steps involved in a comprehensive market feasibility study. These are summarized below, paired with the appraiser's role in each:

1. Product definition: decided by developer and provided to appraiser
2. Market area definition: independently estimated by appraiser
3. Site analysis: independently assessed by appraiser, usually included in a separate chapter of the appraisal report
4. Regional demographics: independently assessed by appraiser, usually included in a separate chapter of the appraisal report
5. Investigation of proposed and existing competition: independently verified or prepared by appraiser
6. Comparison of subject to competition: independently assessed by appraiser
7. Market saturation analysis: independently assessed or prepared by appraiser
8. Primary market research: reviewed by appraiser

9. Conclusions of market feasibility study: independently assessed by appraiser

The key step in a market feasibility analysis is investigating the subject's proposed and existing competition. The appraiser should personally inspect and photograph important comparable facilities. In the report, comparable facilities should be discussed briefly and arrayed on a summary grid, as illustrated in Table 8.1. It is important to compare similar facility types: high-end, for-profit congregate projects with other high-end, for-profit congregate projects; subsidized congregate housing with subsidized congregate housing; personal care with personal care; and CCRCs with CCRCs. If a project contains a combination of housing types—congregate rental housing and personal care, for example, without CCRC characteristics—the appraiser should identify separate competitive facilities for each type.

When comparing the subject to its competition, the appraisal analysis should focus on the characteristics, including both site and development factors, that affect rent or entry fees and absorption rates. Common site characteristics to consider are proximity to retail, medical, and recreational opportunities; access; transportation; and overall neighborhood quality. Common development characteristics include project construction, unit size, unit mix, design, services, management experience, and overall construction quality. The appraiser can compare other facilities to the subject using a traditional "inferior, equal, superior" rating scheme, or quantify differences by arraying each characteristic on a scale of 1 to 5, ranging from "excellent" to "below average." This method helps identify those facilities most comparable to the subject.

Market saturation analysis, discussed in Chapter Seven, is used to measure the overall saturation of elderly housing in a region. The results of this analysis provide the appraiser with additional market evidence to use in estimating market rents and absorption patterns. If the analysis is provided by the developer or outside consultant, the appraiser should review the methods and scenarios used to calculate saturation rates and analyze the reasonableness of the scenarios chosen. Reasonable scenarios would include estimating the total number of senior households for any of three ages—65, 70, and 75—and comparing two income levels—$15,000 and $25,000—for each age group within an appropriate market area. Using parameters below 65 years of age, below a $15,000 income level, or larger than a 30-mile radius would be inappropriate in most instances, except for low-income projects or particularly unique developments.

Appropriate definitions of market area range from five to 30 miles, depending on locational characteristics. An appraiser should make certain that the analysis is calculated consistently. For example, if a market area is defined as extending 20 miles around the site, all competitive facilities within that area should be identified and incorporated in the analysis. It is important to note that developers, appraisers, and lenders have not identified any "correct" or

Table 8.1. Census of Competitive Facilities

No.	Name/Location	Miles From Subject	Year Built	Total Number of Units	Unit Mix	Unit Sizes	Monthly Rent	Rent/ Sq. Ft.	Double Occupancy Surcharge	Occupancy	Number of Meals	Special Features
Comp. 1	The Chateau 2201 Green	6	1979	170	20-Studio 130-1BR 20-2BR	500 700 900	$1,000 1,300 1,600	$2.00 1.86 1.78	$300 300 300	90%	3	None
Comp. 2	Tuliana Gardens 679 Pacific	11	1985	144	36-Studio 108-1BR	425 675	975 1,290	2.29 1.98	225 225	98%	1	Additional Meals Available For Fee
Comp. 3	Presidio Terrace 419 Presidio	17	1983	200	16-Studio 104-1BR 80-2BR	456 660 1,000	1,100 1,400 1,750	2.41 2.12 1.75	275 275 275	83%	2	None
Comp. 4	Ambruster Retirement 2423 Blake	8	Proposed	156	124-1BR 32-2BR	525 775	Unknown	Unknown	Unknown	0%	3	Approved Available 4/87
Subject	Oaknoll Gardens 2201 Pacific	—	Proposed	196	32-Studio 106-1BR 48-2BR	475 600-750 910-960	—	—	—	—	2	Approved Available 4/88

most proper scenarios. The appraiser should use informed, professional judgment and reasonableness in establishing various age, income, and area parameters.

An appraiser should carefully review the results of any primary market research prepared by other parties. Though this information can be persuasive in estimating demand for a project, the appraiser should carefully evaluate sampling methods and the tabulation of results. The strength of this market data depends on the degree of commitment among the potential residents surveyed, which can be seen in their actions. An expression of interest in a survey is not a very reliable indicator of commitment, because seniors can be expected to visit many facilities and weigh their final choices very carefully. Greater degrees of commitment are indicated by, in ascending order, a formal letter of interest, a formal letter of intent, or a deposit. The appraiser should keep in mind, however, that evidence of commitment is not equivalent to actual entry to the facility. Although they are important evidence, even deposits are not conclusive because they are refundable until entry.

The appraiser completes the market analysis section by assessing the development's feasibility. In this conclusion, he or she should consider the subject's competitive market position and any competitive advantages or deficiencies, the results of saturation analysis, primary market research, the project management's level of experience, and the strength and funding of the marketing campaign. These conclusions are used to estimate market rents or fees and absorption patterns in the income capitalization approach section of the appraisal. A well-prepared and researched feasibility analysis will help identify some of the common deficiencies in failed or troubled projects listed below.

- Failure to define target market adequately
- Inadequate feasibility study
- Overly optimistic forecast of absorption pattern and period
- Underestimation of health care costs and annual increases
- Inexperienced architects
- Inexperienced facility operators
- Inadequate allocations to marketing budget or poorly designed marketing programs
- Poor site selection
- Underestimate of annual operating costs
- Inexperienced developers
- Failure to provide for a full continuum of care
- Failure to recognize the specialized nature of elderly housing

Highest and Best Use

Highest and best use is defined as "the reasonably probable and legal use of land or sites as though vacant, found to be physically possible, appropriately supported, financially feasible, and that results in the highest present land value".[1] Appraisers often have difficulties with highest and best use analysis, and senior housing can exacerbate these difficulties because of its special-use nature.

The physical characteristics of the sites used for elderly housing usually do not limit many other types of development. These sites are usually large, enjoy good access, and have necessary site improvements. A site's legally allowable development level is largely influenced by its existing zoning, the potential of rezoning, and the orientation of surrounding development. Most types of elderly housing are developed on sites zoned for high-density residential use. This is appropriate because senior housing is a form a residential development with specialized services. By definition, residential zones do not allow commercial and industrial uses, and rezoning of these areas by community officials is unlikely. However, some projects such as personal care or skilled nursing facilities are probably located in areas of mixed land use or near a medical campus. This may make alternative uses such as professional office or neighborhood commercial development possible.

The feasibility of elderly housing for the subject site is assessed in the market analysis section of the appraisal. In addition to elderly housing, the appraiser should consider any and all physically possible, legally allowable development options that may be feasible for the site. This information can be obtained from regional economic trends and discussions with city officials, developers, brokers, and other appraisers familiar with the region.

Finally, the appraiser considers which use of the land is maximally feasible, given the physical, legal, and financial parameters. In assessing whether elderly housing is maximally feasible, two points should be taken into account. First, senior housing is usually more financially feasible than residential development without age limits, because rents and fees are higher, even after considering increased operating expense ratios. Second, elderly projects are sometimes allowed higher densities and lower parking requirements than conventional housing. This permits a potentially more efficient and profitable use of a site.

The factors discussed above apply to the highest and best use of the site as though vacant. To determine the highest and best use of the site as improved, the appraiser can assess the possibility of higher site densities or lower parking requirements, while keeping in mind what is physically possible, given community approval and market acceptance. In proposing higher densities for a site, the appraiser should take into account the likelihood of a longer absorption period and decreased economies of scale, which would both result in higher operating expenses as a percentage of revenue. For existing projects, the appraiser can analyze the possibilities of rehabilitation, improved maintenance, or better property management.

The highest and best use of the site as though vacant may be different from the highest and best use of the site as improved. This will be true when the

---

[1] *The Dictionary of Real Estate Appraisal* (Chicago: American Institute of Real Estate Appraisers, 1984), p. 152.

existing or proposed improvement is not an optimum use, but makes a contribution to total property value in excess of land value. Highest and best use analysis forms the context for estimating land value, market rents or fees, and possible forms of depreciation used in the cost approach.

9

The Appraisal Process: Valuation

Having collected and analyzed data that influence the market value of the subject property, the appraiser develops value estimates using the applicable approaches: cost, income capitalization, and sales comparison. Because of the specialized nature of elderly housing, the appraiser is likely to encounter practical problems in applying each approach. These special factors are discussed in this chapter. This discussion of the appraisal process considers current appraisal industry standards and financial institution and governmental regulations as appropriate and is in full accordance with them.

Site Valuation

To estimate the market value of the subject site, the appraiser virtually always uses the sales comparison approach, identifying recent sales and listings of vacant land considered somewhat comparable to the subject in location, zoning, and proposed construction. Adjustments are made, if needed, for date of sale, location, terms of sale, and physical characteristics. These adjustments are most often made on a price-per-unit or price-per-square-foot basis.

Our experience in the appraisal of elderly housing suggests that most land used to develop elderly projects has a value approximating vacant, medium- to high-density residential land. This will depend, however, on the site's zoning and location. Exceptions to this include CCRCs, personal care facilities, and skilled nursing facilities, which will sometimes be located in a medical, light office, or institutional zone. Theoretically, vacant land available for its highest and best use as elderly housing is worth more than vacant land available for its highest and best use as conventional, high-density residential development. Higher rents, higher allowed densities, and lower parking requirements are three potential reasons buyers would be willing to pay more for an elderly housing site. However, we have seen insufficient evidence in the market for this hypothesis, except in circumstances where project approvals have been achieved prior to sale.

When searching for comparable land sales data, the appraiser should look for vacant land purchased for elderly housing development. Because only a few of these sales are likely to have occurred, if any, the appraiser will have to identify other high-density residential (or comparably zoned) land sales. When adjusting these sales to the subject, the appraiser should consider differences in density, zoning approvals, and land use restrictions. For example, though the subject site and comparable may be similarly zoned, density bonuses granted for the elderly housing site would suggest an upward adjustment of the comparable in relation to the subject.

Cost Approach

The cost approach is based on the assumption that an informed buyer will pay no more for a property than the cost of producing a substitute property with the same utility. In the cost approach, market value is computed by adding the market value of the land to the direct and indirect replacement costs of the improvements plus entrepreneurial profit, less any type of depreciation. Land value is taken from the site valuation section of the appraisal. Sources for improved replacement costs include

- Cost bids or reported actual construction costs for the subject
- Actual costs of recently constructed comparable properties
- Local contractors' opinions
- A cost service database or manual

Entrepreneurial profit, necessary to motivate the development of real estate, is estimated using the time, money, and risk involved in bringing the property to an income-producing stage. When estimating any accrued depreciation, the appraiser considers such factors as age, condition, functional utility, and detrimental external factors of the property. The total of land costs, direct improvement costs, indirect costs, and entrepreneurial profit is the estimated replacement cost new. Subtracting any required depreciation results in the value of the property by the cost approach.

The cost approach is most applicable to new or proposed properties because few, if any, subjective adjustments for depreciation are needed. Though buyers of real estate rarely rely on the cost approach, it can be used to check the value estimated by the income capitalization approach.

Accurate, detailed estimates of contracting costs, as discussed in Chapter Seven, will incorporate the higher costs involved in developing elderly housing. Experienced cost estimators will be aware of the additional cost of the commons areas, 20% to 50% above unit construction costs on a per-square-foot basis; greater expenditures for furniture and equipment, $1,000 to $5,000 per unit; and specialized unit design. These are only a few of the higher costs incurred in senior developments.

The appraiser must analyze the reasonableness and accuracy of any cost estimate received. This begins with discussions with the cost estimator, along with an assessment of the estimator's experience and knowledge of senior housing. Next, the appraiser can compare incurred or estimated subject construction costs to those for comparable elderly projects. Finally, the appraiser can use a published cost service to verify the accuracy of cost estimates or to approximate roughly the construction costs from scratch. The most commonly used cost service is the Marshall Valuation Service, published by Marshall & Swift. Through this service, an appraiser can estimate the present replacement cost of improvements through a calculator method (total average square footage by building type), a segregated cost method (accumulating average square footage by building component), or cost indexes and multiples (historical costs converted to present-day dollars).

In the calculator method, the Marshall Valuation Service identifies the following housing types related to seniors.

Building Type	Features
Home for the elderly	Congregate housing or personal care units with common areas; specialized unit design; three stories or more
Group care homes	Congregate housing in small buildings that are residential in character; common in small residential care homes
Multiple residences—senior citizen	Noncongregate housing; specialized unit design; two stories or less
Convalescent hospitals	Congregate housing with on-site medical care and therapy

To calculate a subject's replacement cost new, the appraiser must be aware of what the costs listed by the Marshall Valuation Service do not contain. These include

- Sprinkler systems
- Site improvements, including parking
- Off-site costs or public improvements
- Furniture and equipment of commons area
- Marketing costs prior to opening
- Legal and accounting fees necessary to comply with government regulations, such as obtaining a license to operate as a CCRC, residential care, or skilled nursing facility, or creating an enforceable resident occupancy and health care agreement for a CCRC
- Unusual construction and fixtures, such as fireplaces, pools, garden areas, security fencing, or fountains

- Loan fees or points
- Entrepreneurial profit

These costs must be separately identified, estimated, and added to the base costs.

Table 9.1 provides a cost breakdown for a quality 178-unit congregate project located in a moderate climate zone. Cost estimates for CCRCs would include a separate estimate of any skilled nursing and convalescent improvements, higher marketing costs, furniture and equipment, financing fees, and a larger contingency fund.

The Marshall Valuation Service also provides estimates of the average cost per living unit, including the cost of a congregate project's commons area. These are listed below.

Classes A and B	Average: $39,250 per unit Range: $31,500–$49,000
Classes C and D	Average: $30,000 per unit Range: $23,250–$38,500

These costs are estimated before application of any time or location multipliers. Good quality projects located in the western United States generally have a significantly higher cost per unit. Cost schedules for these types of quality projects for congregate, CCRC, and residential care facilities are shown in Tables 9.2, 9.3, and 9.4.

Table 9.1. Cost Approach, Calculator Method

Direct Costs		
Total land value		$ 522,500
Building cost, 155,873 sq. ft. @ $53.15*	$8,284,650	
Landscaping, 150,000 sq. ft. @ $2.50	375,000	
Parking, 73 spaces @ $725	52,925	
Furniture and equipment, 178 units @ $2,274	400,000	
Total direct building costs		+ 9,112,575
Total direct costs (including land)		$ 9,635,075
Legal, accounting and appraisal fees	$ 50,000	
Loan fees	220,000	
Advertising and promotion	100,000	
Operational overhead (5% of building costs)	455,629	
Total indirect costs		+ 825,629
Total construction and land costs		$10,460,704
Plus entrepreneurial profit (15%)		+ 1,569,106
Total cost new (including land)		$12,029,810
Less Depreciation		
Physical curable	$0	
Physical incurable	0	
Functional curable	0	
Functional incurable	0	
External obsolescence	0	
Lease obsolescence	0	
Total depreciation		− 0
Indicated value by the cost approach		$12,029,810, or $12,030,000

	Home for the Elderly, Average to Good, Class D
*Base cost/sq. ft.	$45.99
Sprinkler adjustment	+ 1.25
	$47.24
Current multiplier	× 0.97
	$45.82
Local multiplier	× 1.16
Adjusted base cost/sq. ft.	$53.15

Table 9.2. Actual Project Costs by Unit, Congregate Rental

Facility	Building Costs[1,2]	Furniture & Equipment[2]	Land
A	$85,096	$2,011	$ 4,045
B	15,288	2,424	7,878
C	61,787	2,727	25,181
D	60,096	1,500	9,000
E	94,652	3,797	25,633
F	53,585	2,247	2,935
G	90,478	3,205	17,167
H	63,366	1,868	7,959
J	66,988	2,710	3,554
K	52,328	1,941	7,200
Average	$63,366	$2,443	$12,055

[1] Includes all building hard and soft costs.
[2] Replacement cost new.

Table 9.3. Actual Project Costs by Unit, CCRCs

Facility	Building Costs[1,2]	Furniture & Equipment[2]	Land
A	$49,583	$3,352	$ 7,650
B	50,312	3,690	6,383
C	62,745	3,922	13,725
D	56,711	3,835	8,750
E	213,916	6,726	27,644
Average	$86,665	$4,305	$12,830
	$54,838[3]	$3,700[3]	$ 9,127[3]

[1] Includes all building hard and soft costs.
[2] Replacement cost new.
[3] Averages not considering Facility E.

Table 9.4. Actual Project Costs by Unit, Residential Care

Facility	Building Costs[1,2]	Furniture & Equipment[2]	Land
A	$49,672	$4,500	$ 6,250
B	25,533	6,000	3,643
C	48,377	5,000	2,833
D	48,369	7,360	12,348
E	42,886	3,616	8,600
Average	$42,967	$5,295	$ 6,735

[1] Includes all building hard and soft costs.
[2] Replacement cost new.

In addition to typical direct and indirect costs of a project, there must be an allowance for entrepreneurial profit. This factor is generally derived as a percentage of the development costs, including land. As mentioned above, it represents the compensation to the entrepreneur or developer for the time, money, and risk involved in bringing a project to an income-producing stage. Entrepreneurial profit typically ranges from 10% to 20% and up, depending on the type of property, anticipated absorption or stabilization period, risk, and size of project. An allowance for entrepreneurial profit gives consideration to the going concern value of a project. Because it estimates the level of return on investment capital, the allocation for entrepreneurial profit is useful in assessing the feasibility of a project.

Finally, the appraiser must assess whether an allocation for physical, functional, or external depreciation is necessary. The procedures used to calculate a depreciation deduction are similar to those for any property type, with special focus on potential functional inutilities identified in the "Description of Improvements" section of the appraisal.

Sales Comparison Approach

The sales comparison approach is based on the assumption that an informed buyer will pay no more for a property than the cost of acquiring an existing property with the same utility. The approach is a method of comparing the subject property to recent sales or listings of similar types of retirement properties located in comparable areas. The reliability of a value estimate derived from this approach depends on

- The degree of comparability between the subject and comparable sales
- The length of time since the sales were consummated
- The verifiability and accuracy of the sales data
- The absence of unusual conditions affecting the comparable sales.

Sale prices for successful elderly housing projects usually contain an element for the business' intangible value, such as goodwill. Because this intangible value is difficult to separate from the sale price allocated to the physical real estate, intangible value is not usually identified separately in the sales comparison approach.

Unfortunately, there are typically few transactions involving elderly housing projects. This is a function of the relatively few projects in existence and the newness of many of the existing facilities. Additionally, most successful projects have not been placed on the market. Many of the sales that have occurred have been conducted as a part of bankruptcy or foreclosure proceedings or under duress, making comparability to the subject even more difficult to quantify. For this reason, value estimates using the sales comparison approach are sometimes given little or no weight in the final reconciliation of value.

In most cases, it is not appropriate to use improved sales of conventional apartment developments as comparables because of the significant differences in common areas. Unlike conventional apartments, elderly housing is not a homogeneous property type; each facility is a unique package of location, design, and services.

Sales of improved elderly housing developments are expressed in price per unit, price per bed, or price per square foot. Other indexes could include gross rent multipliers or cost per room. Where sales of reasonably comparable facilities can be located, typical adjustments would include differences in date of sale, terms of sale, age, location, unit sizes, amenities, health care, and project occupancy. Each comparable sale is likely to need significant adjustments. A key adjustment for below-market-rate financing is often necessary when comparing for-profit, conventionally financed comparables with not-for-profit, government-financed comparables. Because of the differences, the appraiser cannot usually attain a precise estimate of value. Instead, the adjusted comparable sales may indicate a range within which the final value determination should fall.

In using the sales comparison approach on a CCRC or development with a combination of services, the appraiser should analyze the congregate residential units, personal care units, and skilled nursing beds as separate markets. Value estimates for each type of housing are then added together to arrive at a total value estimate for the project.

To become aware of those few sales or listings occurring in the illiquid senior housing market, the appraiser should work to develop contacts with developers, lenders, brokers, and other appraisers experienced in the industry. These parties will be the first to know when sales occur. The wave of developers entering the elderly housing industry suggests that, if they can get their developments built, many will be seeking to recoup their investment by offering the projects for sale. This should provide tangible market evidence of improved property sales in the near future.

The discussion of the market sales comparison approach thus far has dealt with the bulk sale to one buyer of all of a project's units. This is appropriate for appraising congregate rental, residential care, and skilled nursing facilities. For buy-in projects such as condominiums, cooperatives, or endowment developments, the sales comparison approach is expanded to estimate not only a bulk-sale market value, but also a retail-sale market value, or the accumulation of individual unit sales to individual buyers. Individual unit sale values are estimated from a market feasibility analysis, as discussed in Chapter Seven. Because there are fewer buy-in senior facilities, the appraiser may be forced to expand the search for comparable unit sales to other geographic areas and similar, but not equal, property types. When comparable unit sale data is weak, subject unit sale prices can be converted to an equivalent monthly rent and compared to rental projects.

To arrive at an estimate of value at the completion of construction, retail-sale market value must be discounted for any selling or operating costs incurred during the absorption period. Recent research suggests that condominium or nonrefundable endowment projects experience a slower absorption of units than either cooperative or rental projects, but this does not take into account a project's competitive advantages or deficiencies.

Income Capitalization Approach

The income capitalization approach is based on the economic principle that the value of a property capable of producing real estate income is equal to the present worth of anticipated future benefits. The annual cash flow or net income projection for a property is converted into a present value estimate using a capitalization process.

There are various methods of capitalization based on inherent assumptions concerning the quality, durability, and pattern of the income stream. The direct capitalization method is based on the application of an overall capitalization rate to a single year's net operating income. This is appropriate for an existing property with a current income equal or close to the stabilized fair market rate.

Where the pattern of projected income is either irregular during the absorption period or simply has not stabilized, discounted cash flow analysis, also known as yield capitalization, is most appropriate. This method is based on the present worth of future cash flow expectancies calculated by individually discounting each anticipated income collection at an appropriate discount rate. The market value attained through this approach is the accumulation of the present worth of each year's projected net income plus the present worth of the reversion. The estimated value of the reversion can be based on a projected appreciation or depreciation of the project value or on a direct capitalization of the reversion year's net income.

Either method—direct capitalization or yield capitalization—will produce a single value estimate that allows for the contribution to value of the real property, such as land and improvements; personal property, such as furniture, fixtures, and equipment; and intangible property, such as goodwill and licenses. Because the contribution of each of these elements is difficult to segregate, their respective contributions to the net cash flow of a project are usually not separately identified and analyzed in the income capitalization approach.

In virtually all circumstances, the income capitalization approach results in the most reliable value estimate for most forms of elderly housing because it most accurately mirrors how investors analyze buying decisions. This means analyzing the project as an ongoing income-producing business or enterprise. The income capitalization approach consists of five basic steps.

1. Selecting the appropriate project period
2. Estimating potential gross income
3. Forecasting annual expenses
4. Selecting an appropriate discount and capitalization rate
5. Applying the proper discounting and capitalization procedures

Projection Period

Projection periods generally range from one year to 15 years. The period should extend to the time at which the property's net income stream becomes stabilized, when both occupancy at market levels and expenses become fixed or established. One-year projection periods can be appropriate for existing properties that have reached a point of stabilized occupancy and expenses. Direct capitalization is applied to the stabilized net income to arrive at an estimate of value.

More typical is a projection period of two to five years, reflecting the normal absorption period of elderly housing. For example, if a development has a 24-month absorption period measured from the completion of construction, the projection period would be 36 months. This is premised on the property owner enjoying the cash flow benefits or deficits of the two-year absorption period, as well as the net proceeds of a hypothetical sale at the end of the second year. The value of the reversion at the end of the 24-month period is based on a direct capitalization of the third year's net income which has stabilized. The theory is that an investor purchasing the property at the end of the second year would be more interested in the anticipated net income in his or her first year of ownership than the previous year's net income under the previous owner. The cash flow of the project's first two years and the value of the reversion are converted to present value for the use of an appropriate discount rate.

For a sophisticated income-producing property, many lenders and developers prefer a traditional 10-year projection period analysis. The appraiser conducts the same calculations described above, discounting the annual cash flows for the first 10 years of the project and discounting the value of the reversion, which is the direct capitalization of the projected eleventh-year income. Longer projection periods, up to 15 years or more, are sometimes necessary for CCRCs, because many of these facilities do not become actuarially stabilized until the 10th to 15th year. Due to resident turnover from death, relocation, or sale, the total resident population, and therefore the net cash flows from refundable entry deposits, does not stabilize until that time.

Projecting absorption periods and patterns for senior housing is difficult and imprecise. Past history of even comparable properties may give an inaccurate indication of absorption merely because of demographics. In estimating the absorption period, the appraiser should consider

- The number of units to be absorbed
- The occupancy rates and waiting lists at comparable facilities
- Actuarial patterns of comparable projects
- Any competitive advantages or deficiencies that may influence the subject's position in its competitive environment
- Results of market saturation analysis
- Results of primary market research

- Experience of developers
- Depth of marketing campaign

Our experience indicates the following absorption patterns for an average 170-unit facility.

	Average	Range
Preleasing	20%	0 to 50%
Absorption pattern	6-7 units per month	4-5 to 10-12 units per month
Absorption period	18-24 months	12-60 months

These averages may not reflect patterns in highly competitive markets.

An appraiser will usually assume an even absorption pattern during the absorption period, but actual market experience shows that absorption is usually not even. A higher percentage of units will rent out in the early months of the project, and the remaining units will stretch out the absorption period. But forecasting an uneven absorption pattern is often more difficult to support than a conservative estimate of an equal or regular absorption pattern.

Potential Gross Income

Potential gross income is the maximum rent or revenue that a facility can achieve, given its competitive market position. Market rents or fees are drawn from the analysis of existing and proposed comparable projects in the market feasibility study. The appraiser can summarize the results of this survey using a range, average, and most comparable rent-per-square-foot grid.

The appraiser should objectively evaluate the subject's competitive advantages and disadvantages when estimating market rents. This can only be accomplished through an exhaustive review of similar property types. Appraisers quantify the comparison of the subject to other projects using an adjustment grid, adjusting each in relation to the subject. Using monthly rent-per-square-foot figures and grouping them by unit type, the appraiser can adjust for age, location, project construction, unit design, amenities, and overall quality. After all adjustments have been made, the comparables should theoretically reflect an approximate market rent for the subject.

Other Considerations

Conclusions reached in a survey of competitive properties can be supported by the results of primary market research. This research can provide the direct market evidence needed to support proposed rent levels for the subject. Often, a proposed project, particularly a high-end congregate facility, will not be directly comparable to any existing facilities within the primary market area.

Most projects being developed today are of a higher quality and seek higher rents than earlier generations of elderly housing projects. Though common sense suggests that a higher quality facility can command higher rents, this is often hard to quantify. Proposed rents that are above the market average must be linked to market evidence. Sometimes the appraiser will need to go outside the primary market area to locations with similar demographics and economics to find market support for higher quality properties. Though these facilities do not compete directly with the subject, they provide evidence for market acceptance of higher rents in exchange for higher quality.

Double Occupancy

Most elderly housing developments levy surcharges for a second occupant. These extra rents or fees can be estimated from comparable projects or from the cost of providing additional meals to a second occupant. The level of double occupancy at any project depends primarily on unit sizes and the orientation of the development's tenant mix. The double occupancy rate ranges from zero to 50%; roughly broken down by unit type, the rate is 0%-20% for studios, 10%-50% for one-bedrooms, and 50%-90% for two bedrooms. Facilities offering living assistance or medical care will have smaller units and therefore fewer couples, while projects oriented to recreation will have larger units and more couples.

Miscellaneous Income

Many elderly projects offer extra amenities that are not included in the resident's monthly rent or maintenance fee. Offering services on a "fee-for-service" basis is an increasingly common way to tailor services and their costs to the individual desires of each resident. The fee-for-service system can be implemented for meals, housekeeping, living assistance, or medical care. When comparing the subject to competitive facilities that are not fee-for-service, the appraiser must convert these extra fees to equivalent monthly rents or maintenance fees. Other sources of miscellaneous income include guest rooms, guest meals, parking, laundry, and specialized health or beauty treatment services. Miscellaneous income can range from zero to 5% of potential gross income, depending on the extent of a project's fee-for-service policy.

Endowment fees representing one-time, nonrefundable entry surcharges are another source of miscellaneous income for congregate rental projects. Though many rental projects have encountered market opposition even to small entry fees, some developers feel that aggressive marketing campaigns can overcome this and make entry fees acceptable. The appraiser should gauge market acceptance for these fees carefully by converting them to equivalent monthly rents before comparison to competitive facilities. Through superior quality, extra amenities, or an effective marketing campaign, a congregate rental development can gain market acceptance for entry fees.

Vacancy and Collection Losses

Vacancy and collection losses must be deducted from all revenue sources to arrive at an estimate of effective gross income. These deductions represent absorption period vacancies, vacancies from normal unit turnover after stabilization, and rent collection delinquencies or delays. Since elderly housing tends to have lower turnover and fewer collection problems than conventional rental housing, deductions typically range from 2% to 5% of potential gross income after stabilization. Turnover experience tabulated by Laventhol & Horwath is illustrated in Table 9.5.

Table 9.5. Annual Apartment Turnover (per 100 Residents)[1]

	Deaths		Permanent Transfers to Nursing Center		Total Turnover		
	Males	Females	Males	Females	Males	Females	Combined[2]
Principally retirement center							
Pre-1975 facilities:							
1985	8.4	6.0	5.4	4.5	14.8	10.8	12.0
1984	9.1	5.7	5.6	5.3	14.7	10.7	11.5
1983	7.2	5.4	4.3	4.6	11.5	10.0	10.3
1975 and later facilities:							
1985	8.9	3.8	2.1	3.4	12.1	7.9	8.8
1984	5.4	3.5	4.3	2.9	9.7	6.4	7.1
1983	8.1	3.1	2.5	2.4	10.6	5.5	6.6
Oriented toward nursing care							
Pre-1975 facilities:							
1985	4.8	3.6	9.2	5.4	14.4	9.0	10.1
1984	7.0	2.8	9.1	12.5	16.1	15.3	15.6
1983	10.7	4.1	12.1	12.1	22.8	16.2	18.8

[1] All amounts are medians.
[2] Taking into consideration previously stated proportion of females and males for each year.
SOURCE: Laventhol & Horwath, *The Senior Living Industry, 1986*, p. 42. Reprinted with permission.

Effective Gross Income

Effective gross income is the anticipated income from all sources less the vacancy and collection loss allowance. Components of effective gross income are illustrated by major senior housing type below.

Congregate Rental:

Gross rental income

Double-occupancy surcharges

Miscellaneous income

Less vacancy and collection losses

Effective gross income

Residential Care:

Private rooms—market income

Semiprivate rooms—market income

SSI rooms income

Miscellaneous income

Less vacancy and collection losses

Effective gross income

Skilled Nursing Care:

Medicare revenues

Medicaid revenues

Private pay revenues

Ancillary revenues

Miscellaneous income

Less vacancy and collection losses

Less deductions from revenue

Effective gross income

Operating Expenses

Operating expenses are the periodic expenditures necessary to maintain the subject and continue the production of effective gross income. Operating expenses are estimated on a cash basis and do not include capital expenditures, one-time expenditures, expenses unique to a particular management, debt service, depreciation, or income taxes.

Operating expenses consist of three components: fixed expenses, variable expenses, and reserves for replacements. Fixed expenses are operating expenses that generally do not vary with occupancy and are incurred whether the project is full or vacant. These commonly include real estate taxes and insurance. These expenses can vary, but they are not dependent on a facility's occupancy level. They can be estimated from historical operating data or discussions with local assessors and insurance agents.

Variable expenses include all expenditures that vary with occupancy or the intensity of property operation. They represent the majority of operating expenses, including management, general and administrative, utilities, maintenance, activities, transportation, marketing, housekeeping, dietary, personal care, and medical care. These expenses can vary substantially from year to year, though they generally stabilize as a percentage of effective gross income. Variable expenses can be estimated by three methods: a line-by-line budget basis, cost per unit or per resident, or as a percentage of effective gross income.

Replacement reserves are allocations providing for the periodic replacement of building and equipment components that wear out more rapidly than the building itself. The annual reserve allocation is estimated from the cost of replacement prorated over the remaining life of the building component. These components can include roof areas, carpeting, all furniture and equipment, and landscaping.

Table 9.6 summarizes the nature of typical operating expenses.

Table 9.6. Operating Expenses

Operating Expense	Description	Fixed or Variable	Methods of Estimating
Real Estate Taxes	Annual real estate taxes for land, improvements and personal property	Fixed	Operating history, public records, assessor's office
Insurance	Fire, malpractice, liability	Fixed	Operating history, insurance agents
Management	Contractual specialized management fee	Variable	Percentage of EGI, line-by-line budget, per unit/resident, from comparable projects, experienced housing operators
Utilities	Electricity, gas, water	Variable	Same as above
Maintenance	Janitorial and grounds, payroll and benefits, elevator contracts, supplies, garbage removals	Semi-variable	Same as above
Activities	Social programs, personnel payroll and benefits, supplies, program costs	Variable	Same as above
Transportation	Van leasing, oil and gas, repair	Semi-variable	Same as above
Marketing	On-going promotional expenditures, advertising, brochures	Semi-variable	Same as above
Housekeeping	Manager and staff, payroll and benefits, supplies, laundry	Variable	Same as above
Dietary	Managers and staff, payroll and benefits, supplies, raw cost of food	Variable	Same as above
Personal Care & Medical Care	Manager and staff, payroll and benefits, supplies, medication, professional fees	Variable	Same as above

After estimating all expenses on a line-by-line basis, the appraiser should examine the estimate of total expenses relative to the size of the development and percentage of effective gross income. The appraiser should use his or her judgment, experience, and knowledge of comparable developments to evaluate the reasonableness of the total operating expenses. Our experience supports the following operating expense guidelines.

Facility Type	Typical Size	Expenses as a % of EGI	Expenses per Unit
Congregate rental	120–250 units	40%–55%	$ 4,000–9,000
Personal care	30–50 beds	50%–70%	$ 4,500–10,000
Skilled nursing	50–99 beds	70%–85%	$10,000–25,000

These ranges are dependent on a project's total development size, rent level, and location. Expense ratios for actual congregate rental and residential care projects are shown in Tables 9.7 and 9.8.

Table 9.7. Operating Expenses, Congregate Rental

Facility	Total Expenses	Number of Units	Expenses/ Unit	Expense as % of EGI
A	$ 838,257	120	$6,985	46.3%
B	926,151	120	7,718	52.2
C	1,165,391	150	7,769	46.4
D	1,111,348	174	6,387	43.2
E	1,209,832	200	6,049	44.7
F	1,044,963	172	6,075	43.9
G	1,115,739	178	6,268	43.6
H	2,096,570	272	7,708	44.8
I	1,549,112	219	7,073	44.7
J	1,204,514	196	6,145	42.3
Average	$1,226,187	180	$6,818	45.2%

Table 9.8. Operating Expenses, Residential Care

Facility	Total Expenses	Number of Units	Number of Beds	Expenses/ Bed	Expense as % of EGI
A	$526,231	52	94	$5,598	58.8%
B	265,475	30	60	4,424	65.0
C	179,517	14	28	6,411	64.2
D	101,750	9	15	6,783	64.3
E	415,091	32	70	5,930	67.3
Average	$297,613	27	53	$5,829	63.9%

Capitalization Rates

A capitalization rate is a factor that represents the relationship between one year's net income and the property's present value. The rate is expressed as a decimal factor, which is divided into the net income and results in an estimate of value by the income capitalization approach.

$$\text{Present value} = \frac{\text{Net operating income}}{\text{Capitalization rate}}$$

Capitalization rates can be derived from studying comparable sales, analyzing the nature of elderly housing in relation to other property types, using a band-of-investment technique, investment surveys, and interviews with developers, brokers, and lenders familiar with elderly housing.

Ideally, capitalization rates used in the appraisal of elderly housing are drawn from the sale of other comparable projects. Unfortunately, few arm's-length, nonduress sales of senior housing developments have occurred to date. The combination of few sales, lack of comparability, and insufficiently reliable income data to compute the rates usually forces the appraiser to rely on other methods. One method is for the appraiser to compare capitalization rates directly to property types in more liquid markets for which rates are more easily derived. For example, congregate rental developments can be thought of as a combination of a conventional apartment complex providing shelter and a hotel offering on-site services. Capitalization rates of 8% to 9% for apartments and 11% to 13% for hotels would indicate an approximate rate of 10% to 11% for congregate rental projects. Appraisers should realize that this method of estimating capitalization rates is qualitative and only suggests a range by elderly housing type. It also does not consider specific project characteristics in relation to that project's immediate competition.

The band-of-investment technique is based on the assumption that most properties are purchased with debt and equity capital and that each investment position requires a market-determined return on investment. This return includes a competitive interest rate to the debt-holder or lender and a competitive equity yield to the equity investor or developer. Band-of-investment calculations are illustrated below.

Component	Ratio		Rate		Rate Component
Mortgage	Loan-to-value ratio	×	Mortgage constant	=	Weighted average of debt
Equity	Equity-to-value ratio	×	Equity dividend rate	=	Weighted average of equity
			Total	=	Overall capitalization rate

Typically, high loan-to-value ratios of 70% to 85% make capitalization rates very sensitive to mortgage conditions. While mortgage information is readily available, it is often a difficult and imprecise process to estimate an equity dividend rate that reflects the higher risks involved in elderly housing. Sources likely to be helpful to the appraiser include developers, brokers, and lenders familiar with this type of project. These parties are often aware of capitalization rate ranges for various elderly housing types. The appraiser must then assess the advantages, disadvantages, and risks inherent in the subject property itself to estimate properly the subject's likely capitalization rate within the range. Our experience supports the following capitalization rate ranges.

Congregate rental, low-end	8.5%–10%
Congregate rental, high-end	9.5%–11.5%
Personal care facility	10%–12%
Skilled nursing facility	12%–15%
CCRC	10%–13%

The higher capitalization rates for the more intensive personal care and skilled nursing facilities reflect the higher risks and specialized management associated with those more unique property types.

Discount Rates

Discount rates are factors applied to annual net operating cash flows and to the property's future or reversion value to arrive at an estimate of net present value. The rates are comprised of the annual cash-on-cash return or equity divided rate plus an estimate of the property's yearly appreciation rate, less the annual inflation rate. Discount rates for elderly housing are also influenced by investors' expectations in this market. In our experience, discount rates for elderly housing approximate 12% to 16%, depending on the quality of the subject's estimated income stream, the forecasted length of the absorption period, and the degree of investment risk. Discount rates are usually higher than capitalization rates because cash flows during the absorption period are more variable and subject to wrong estimates than stabilized cash flows.

Capitalization Process

Most proposed projects today are being appraised as of the completion of construction, before they have reached stabilized occupancy. In these cases, the appraiser first estimates the value at stabilized occupancy by capitalizing the net income in the stabilized year. This reversion value and the cash flows during the absorption period are then discounted to the end of the construction period using a discount rate or rates. Pro forma capitalized income and expense statements are illustrated in Chapter 10 for both proposed and existing elderly housing projects.

Reconciliation Process

Once value estimates have been made using the three approaches, the appraiser must reconcile these figures for a final determination of value. The development of a final estimate of value involves a careful, logical analysis of the procedures leading to each indication of value and the appraiser's judgment of the appropriateness, accuracy, and quantity of evidence.

In most cases, the final value determination derived by using the income capitalization approach is most appropriate. This approach most closely resembles the analysis performed by investors and buyers of this type of specialized property. It also incorporates all components of a project's value, including the value of physical real estate and business value. The sales comparison approach is usually given less weight because of the lack of comparable sales and large differences between projects. The cost approach, though appropriate for new or proposed developments, is rarely relied on by investors in this type of property.

10

Case Studies

The case studies of proposed and existing elderly housing presented in this chapter are designed to illustrate valuation methods and recommended formats for pro forma revenue and expense estimates. They also show the relationships between various project characteristics and valuation conclusions. The narrative discussion for each case study emphasizes, in limited detail, a particular aspect of the valuation of elderly housing. Although the case studies involve large, sophisticated developments generally located in a region of high land and construction costs, the interrelationships between various project elements and valuation statistics are valid for smaller projects in less costly locations. Even though our examples emphasize valuation using the income capitalization approach, an appraiser should consider estimates derived from the cost and sales comparison approaches as well before making a final value determination.

Great care should be exercised by those using case study figures for the analysis of an existing or proposed senior project. Our experience suggests that significant differences in project characteristics, location, management, and competitive environments exist that greatly affect value estimates. Appraisers are encouraged to gather and examine additional case studies of projects that are more comparable to subject properties.

This chapter will outline and discuss the following projects:

Case Study A—Illustration of market saturation analysis for a proposed 156-unit congregate rental project. Emphasis will be placed on analysis methodology.

Case Study B—Project and valuation statistics for a proposed 174-unit congregate rental project. Emphasis will be on estimating pro forma income and expenses.

Case Study C—Project and valuation statistics for a proposed 192-unit continuing-care retirement community. Emphasis will be on forecasting components of potential gross income.

Case Study D—Project and valuation statistics for an existing combined 220-unit congregate rental and 45-unit residential care project. Emphasis will be on the determination of an appropriate capitalization rate.

Case Study A

Project Description

Facility A is a proposed 156-unit congregate rental project located in a rapidly growing metropolitan area in the western United States. The development, to be built on a six-acre site, will consist of one three-story, wood-frame residential structure connected to a one-story, wood-frame community building. Improvements comprise 143,000 square feet of the gross building area. The project will offer three meals daily, weekly housekeeping, and both indoor and outdoor recreational areas. Proposed monthly rents range from $1,000 for a 575-square-foot, one-bedroom unit to $1,400 for an 850-square-foot, two-bedroom unit. Facility A is located in a predominantly residential neighborhood with nearby retail and medical services. The metropolitan area is evolving from its historical origins as an agricultural center to a diversified community with a service-oriented economy.

Market Area Definition

Facility A's metropolitan area, with a population of 120,000, is the demographic, economic, and approximate geographic center of a largely agricultural county of 300,000 people. The county jurisdiction extends approximately 25 miles in all directions from the subject site. The county's boundaries form the subject's primary market area. This distance represents a reasonable driving distance for friends and relatives. Demand for the subject may be augmented by seniors living outside the county, but this secondary market demand is affected by other comparable facilities located outside the subject's primary market area.

Competitive Supply

During the course of the market analysis, all existing and proposed facilities considered somewhat comparable to the subject were identified, including all for-profit, market-rate congregate senior facilities. Subsidized elderly housing and projects offering on-site medical care were not included. The analysis showed one existing facility of 72 units, generally inferior to the subject property in project construction and services. Discussions with county officials also uncovered an additional, proposed 172-unit project seeking government approval. Therefore, the total supply of existing and proposed comparable projects was 244 units without considering the subject and 400 units in total.

112

Forecast Demand

To measure the theoretical size of the subject's target market, demographic statistics extracted from the 1980 U.S. census were analyzed for the relevant target market area. Also obtained were 1986 population estimates and 1991 projections for this area. These data are illustrated in Table 10.1.

Table 10.1. Case Study A, Number of Households

Primary Market Area—County
Households Age 65 and Older

Income Level	Age 65 to 74	Age 75 and older	Age 65 and older
1980 U.S. Census—			
$15,000–$25,000	3,831	1,036	4,867
$25,000 and above	1,019	314	1,437
Total	4,850	1,350	6,304
1986 Estimate—			
$15,000–$25,000	4,313	1,133	5,446
$25,000 and above	1,437	457	1,894
Total	5,750	1,590	7,340
1991 Projection—			
$15,000–$25,000	4,629	1,230	5,159
$25,000 and above	1,800	562	2,362
Total	6,429	1,792	8,221

The market saturation rate calculations, shown in Table 10.2, were made in the following manner.

1. The number of senior households over a minimum age—65 or 75— and a minimum income requirement—$15,000 or $25,000—sufficient to pay proposed monthly rentals were determined. These variables establish the different scenarios for calculating market penetration rates.
2. The total market saturation rates required to fill the subject's proposed 156 units and all other existing and proposed competitive projects were calculated.
3. The feasibility of the subject given the calculated rates was considered and analyzed.

Table 10.2. Case Study A, Market Saturation Analysis

| | Number of Households | Saturation Rates[1] | | |
		w/o Subject (244 units)	w/Subject (400 units)	Only Subject (156 units)
1986 Estimate				
65+, $15,000+	7,340	3.3%	5.5%	2.2%
75+, $15,000+	1,590	15.4%	25.2%	4.8%
65+, $25,000+	1,894	12.9%	21.2%	8.2%
75+, $25,000+	457	53.4%	87.5%	34.1%
1991 Projection				
65+, $15,000+	8,221	3.0%	4.9%	1.9%
75+, $15,000+	1,792	13.6%	22.3%	8.7%
65+, $25,000+	2,362	10.3%	16.9%	6.6%
75+, $25,000+	562	43.4%	71.2%	27.8%

[1] Market saturation rates represent the total market demand which is necessary to absorb
  a) existing and proposed units *not* including the subject.
  b) existing and proposed units including the subject.
  c) *only* the subject units.

Comments

As discussed in Chapter Six, a market saturation rate of 15% or more indicates a speculative estimate of market demand. In this case study, rates of 15% or less are met only in the most broad and inclusive scenarios. This illustrates the shallowness of the senior market in smaller metropolitan areas like the subject region. Though the paucity of existing facilities suggests an underbuilt market, this unmet demand can be absorbed by only one or two proposed projects. The calculated penetration rates indicate that, if the comparable proposed 172-unit project is constructed, the subject may be a speculative venture.

For the subject to be successful, the sponsor must consider an aggressive, well-funded marketing campaign aimed at seniors aged 65 to 75. The developer should analyze the effect of possibly lower rents and an extended absorption period if the proposed competition is built. In any event, the subject sponsor should proceed expeditiously through the development process to gain competitive advantages over other proposed projects.

As discussed earlier, while saturation analysis can measure the overall saturation of elderly housing within a market area, it does not incorporate the competitive advantages or deficiencies of a particular project. Lower rents, above-average services, or creative, well-funded marketing programs are all possible methods of overcoming saturated markets. This illustration of market saturation analysis is only part of the larger market analysis which documents competitive properties, compares competitive properties to the subject, analyzes the results of any primary market research, and determines the feasibility of the subject property.

Case Study B

Project Description

Facility B is a proposed, 174-unit congregate rental project located in a rapidly growing metropolitan area in the western United States. The development, to be built on a 7.4-acre site, will consist of one two-story, wood-frame residential structure attached to a one-story, wood-frame community building. The complex will offer three meals daily, weekly housekeeping, and both indoor and outdoor recreation spaces.

Facility B is located in a residential neighborhood and is a sufficient distance from major retail and medical facilities, though adjacent to a golf course. This project's metropolitan area, with a population of 50,000, is an agricultural trade and distribution center. To date, the project's primary market area extends to a radius of about 20 miles and is characterized by limited direct competition. Calculated market saturation rates, including the subject, range from 5% to 10%.

Pro Forma Income and Expense

The valuation of Facility B using the income capitalization approach requires the following key steps in the development of a pro forma income and expense schedule.

1. Estimate of absorption period and pattern
2. Determination of a subject market rent by unit type
3. Forecast of expenses in the stabilized year and during the absorption period

Absorption Period and Pattern. With 174 units, the subject's will be the largest retirement community in its primary market area and therefore represents a significant addition to the supply of retirement units in the area. The calculated saturation rates of 5% to 10% indicate a general undersupply of retirement apartment units. Actual market experience in other regions suggests that good-quality, competitively priced projects typically experience stabilized occupancy within 18 to 24 months after completion. The estimate of a 24-month absorption period for the subject, which is at the upper end of the typical range, is appropriate because the subject's 174 units are slightly above average for a congregate rental development. Also, the relatively small population of the primary market area and presently light competitive market hint that extensive exposure and marketing will be necessary to create demand for a high-quality housing option such as the subject. The following absorption pattern can be calculated from these estimates.

Total units	174	
Preleased units (25%)	− 44	
Units to be leased at completion of construction	130	
Absorption period	÷ 24	months
Absorption rate	5.4 units/month	

Table 10.3. Case Study B, Project and Valuation Statistics

Project Statistics	
Units	174
Rooms	372
Unit sizes—(sq. ft.)	
24—studios	460
126—1 bedroom	570-630
24—2 bedrooms	805
Total building area (sq. ft.)	164,860
Building area/unit (sq. ft.)	947
Land area (sq. ft.)	322,344
Land area/Unit (sq. ft.)	1,853
Valuation Statistics	
Land value/unit	$ 4,046
Improvement cost/unit	$55,097
Improvement cost/sq. ft.	$ 58.15
F F & E/unit	$ 2,011
Monthly rental—	
Studio	$ 475 ($2.12/sq. ft.)
1 bedroom	$ 1,150 ($1.92/sq. ft.)
2 bedroom	$ 1,250 ($1.55/sq. ft.)
Average monthly revenue/unit	$ 1,139
Vacancy allowance	4%
Miscellaneous income	1%
Absorption period	24 mos.
Preleasing percentage	20%
Double occupancy percentage	27.6%
Operating expense/unit	$ 6,435
Operating expense percentage	43.7%
Discount rate	15%
Capitalization rate	10%
Total value/unit	$82,830
Total value/room	$38,743
Total value/sq. ft.	$ 87.42
Discount for absorption period	17.4%

Market Rent. The survey of competitive properties noted four developments that were somewhat competitive to the subject. Each of these facilities, though offering a similar amenities package, is an older facility with smaller, fewer units. Market rents for these existing facilities are 10% to 20% less than those projected for the subject. To better estimate a market rent for the subject units, a supplemental market analysis of congregate rental units outside the subject's primary market area was conducted. Although these projects are not likely to compete directly with the subject due to differences in distance, they provide evidence of market acceptance for higher rents for newer, higher-quality projects with larger unit sizes. It was found that forecasting higher rents for the subject was reasonable after considering the subject's newness, higher quality, and larger unit sizes. Uncertainty over forecast subject market rents is a factor in estimating a higher-than-average discount rate used to discount pro forma cash flows during the absorption period.

In this pro forma income and expense estimate, market rents derived above are forecast during the two-year absorption period. Market rents are increased 5% in the first year of stabilization, which is the third year after the completion of construction. This increase reflects the forecast full occupancy achieved for the subject, trends of rents in the region, and general inflationary trends and expectations.

Expenses. Pro forma expenses in the three-year projection period were estimated using the following information.

- Experience with similar projects
- Discussions with the proposed project operators regarding their estimate of expenses
- Evaluation of the impact of specific factors of location, quality, and the proposed amenities package on specific expenses

In general, expenses were estimated in the first year of stabilization—Year Three—and then forecast during the two-year absorption period. This analysis involved a line-by-line analysis of the nature of each item. For example, strictly variable expenses such as management fees are a simple percentage of effective gross income each year and were estimated at 5% annually. Other expenses such as dietary costs are semivariable. Specifically, dietary expenses were estimated as 17.27% in the stabilized year. This expense was decreased by 10% for Year Two (80% occupancy) and 40% for Year One (40% occupancy), reflecting the semivariable nature of dietary expense. A complete breakdown of income and expenses is shown in Table 10.4, while discounted cash flows for the project are shown in Table 10.5.

Comments

Our experience in appraising senior housing suggests that Facility B is a typical congregate rental development in terms of average project construction and the unit mix, service package, and overall project development risk. Proposed rents were supported by existing projects within the primary market area.

While building improvement costs, land costs, and operating expenses are slightly lower than comparable facilities located in major metropolitan areas, this reflects the region's relatively lower cost of living.

Table 10.4. Case Study B, Pro Forma Income and Expenses

	Year 1	Year 2	Year 3
Average occupancy	40%	80%	100%
Average rental	$ 1,134	$ 1,139	$ 1,196
Potential gross income—			
24 studios @ $975/mo.	$ 112,320	$ 224,640	$ 294,840
126 1 bedrooms @ $1,150/mo.	695,520	1,391,040	1,825,740
24 2 bedrooms @ $1,250/mo.	144,000	288,000	378,000
	$ 951,840	$1,903,680	$2,498,580
Double occupancy—			
19 units @ $250/mo.	57,000		
38 units @ $250/mo.		114,000	
48 units @ $250/mo.			144,000
Miscellaneous income	4,518	19,037	24,986
Total gross income	$1,018,358	$2,036,717	$2,667,566
Less: vacancy & collection losses			
Year 1—1%	(10,184)		
Year 2—2%		(40,734)	
Year 3—4%			(106,703)
Effective Gross Income	$1,008,174	$1,995,983	$2,560,863
Expenses			
Real estate taxes	$ 110,000	$ 115,500	$ 121,275
Insurance	47,165	49,523	52,000
Management	50,409	99,799	128,043
G & A	39,619	53,486	82,400
Activities	12,000	19,000	21,000
Marketing	50,000	37,500	25,000
Utilities	63,129	99,429	116,000
Maintenance	43,084	45,236	47,500
Transportation	26,667	28,000	29,400
Housekeeping	44,408	69,943	81,600
Dietary	198,857	313,200	365,400
Replacement reserves	50,000	50,000	50,000
Total expenses	$ 735,338	$ 980,618	$1,119,618
	(72.9%)	(40.1%)	(43.7%)
Net income	$ 272,836	$1,015,365	$1,441,245

Table 10.5. Case Study B, Discounted Cash Flow

	Year 1	Year 2	Year 3
Net income	$272,836	$1,015,365	$ 1,441,245
Capitalization rate	—	—	.10
Capitalized value	—	—	$14,412,450
Discount factor	.8696	.7561	.7561
Discounted value	$237,258	$ 767,717	$10,897,253

Recap	
Year 1	$ 237,258
Year 2	767,717
Year 3	10,897,253
Total Discounted Value	$11,902,228
Total Stabilized Value	$14,412,450

Case Study C

Project Description

Facility C is a proposed 192-unit continuing-care retirement community located in a small city on the West Coast. The campus-like complex consists of 150 congregate apartment units, 12 residential care units with a total of 20 beds, and 30 skilled nursing units with a total of 50 beds. The project will offer congregate housing and lifetime medical care memberships in exchange for a 90% refundable endowment, payable upon entry, and a monthly maintenance fee. The facility's residential care and skilled nursing units are first available to members at no additional cost. However, the operator will seek nonmember residents to maintain full occupancy in the residential care and skilled nursing beds. All residents will receive three meals daily, weekly maid service, and full indoor recreational activities.

The complex, to be built on a 6.3-acre site, will contain 10 separate buildings. The project's commons area, residential care units, and skilled nursing units are each contained in separate though adjoining one-story, wood-frame improvements. Congregate apartment units are contained in seven one- and two-story, wood-frame buildings.

Facility C is located in a neighborhood of compatible, high-density residential land uses. Neighborhood retail facilities are located in close proximity to the site, with major medical care only two miles away. The project's metropolitan area has a population of 43,000 and is a self-contained community with extensive outdoor recreational facilities. The subject's primary market, extending to a radius of approximately 25 miles, reaches into the suburbs of a major metropolitan area. This market area is characterized by increasing direct competition to the subject. Calculated market saturation rates range from 10% to 15%.

Table 10.6. Case Study C, Project and Valuation Statistics

Project Statistics

Congregate apartment units	150
Residential care units (beds)	12 (20)
Skilled nursing units (beds)	30 (50)
Total units (occupants)	192 (220)
Total rooms	417
Unit sizes—(sq. ft.)	
75—1 bedrooms	750 avg.
75—2 bedrooms	1,000 avg.
12—residential care	290
30—skilled nursing	260
Total building area (sq. ft.)	182,443
Building area/unit (sq. ft.)	950
Land area (sq. ft.)	272,865
Land area/unit (sq. ft.)	1,420

Valuation Statistics

Land value/unit	$ 7,292
Improvement cost/unit	$ 67,130
Improvement cost/sq. ft.	$ 70.65
F F & E/unit	$ 3,196
Endowment fee—	
1 bedroom	$90,000 ($1.20/sq. ft.)
2 bedroom	$120,000 ($1.20/sq. ft.)
Monthly maintenance fee—1st person	$ 1,000
Monthly maintenance fee—2nd person	$ 350
Residential care	$1,500/month
Skilled nursing	$70/day
Absorption period	36 mos.
Preleasing	50%
Double occupancy percentage	30%
Vacancy allowance	5%
Apartment expense/unit	$ 7,000
Residential care expense/unit	$ 9,000
Skilled nursing expense/unit	$ 15,000
Appreciation rates—	
Endowment fees	4%
Maintenance fees	4%
Skilled nursing rate	4%
Residential care rate	4%
Operating expenses	4%
Residential care expenses	4%
Skilled nursing expenses	4%
Discount rate	11.5%
Capitalization rate	12%
Value/unit	$116,503
Value/room	$ 53,647
Value/sq. ft.	$ 122.62

Components of Potential Gross Income

The valuation of a CCRC using the income capitalization approach is uniquely difficult due to the several components of potential gross income. An appraiser must estimate revenue from

- Endowment receipts
- Endowment resale income
- Reserve fund interest income
- Monthly maintenance revenues for first and second residents under plan
- Skilled nursing revenue from nonmembers
- Residential care revenue from nonmembers

Estimates of annual income and expenses are shown in Table 10.7.

Endowment Receipts. Endowment receipts are the one-time entry fees received from initial project residents. The endowment fee for the subject is estimated using methods similar to estimating any source of revenue, that is, comparison with similar facilities through a comprehensive market feasibility analysis. This analysis resulted in an estimate of initial endowment fees for the subject of $90,000 for a one-bedroom unit and $120,000 for two bedrooms. Initial endowment receipts are calculated below.

Period	Average Endowment Fee	Forecasted Absorption Pattern	Initial Endowment Receipts
Preopening	$105,000	75 units	$7,875,000
Year 1	$105,000	25 units	$2,625,000
Year 2	$105,000	25 units	$2,625,000
Year 3	$105,000	25 units	$2,625,000

Table 10.7. Case Study C, Pro Forma Income & Expenses

	Pre-Opening	Year 1	Year 2	Year 3	Year 4
Potential gross annual income—					
Endowment receipts	$7,875,000	$2,625,000	$2,625,000	$2,625,000	$ —
Endowment resale income		—	21,000	42,000	88,200
Reserve fund investment income		—	36,750	74,970	114,719
Monthly maintenance fee—1st person		1,050,000	1,374,000	1,722,000	2,021,760
Monthly maintenance fee—2nd person		69,300	140,700	168,000	187,824
Skilled nursing revenue—nonmembers		1,200,850	1,195,740	1,105,395	977,143
Residential care revenue—nonmembers		324,000	262,080	175,219	101,213
Other revenue		75,000	100,286	127,474	139,063
Total gross income	$7,875,000	$5,344,150	$5,755,556	$6,040,058	$3,629,922
Less: vacancy & collection losses		(52,883)	(148,626)	(158,556)	(164,397)
Effective gross income	$7,875,000	$5,291,267	$5,606,930	$5,881,502	$3,465,525
Expenses—					
Departmental operating expenses		$1,102,500	$1,328,600	$1,571,010	$1,732,186
Residential care expenses		40,000	41,600	43,264	44,995
Skilled nursing care expenses		400,000	416,000	432,640	449,946
Reserve fund		525,000	546,000	567,840	590,554
Replacement reserves		100,000	100,000	100,000	100,000
Total expenses		$2,167,500	$2,432,200	$2,714,754	$2,917,681
Net income	$7,875,000	$3,123,767	$3,174,730	$3,166,748	$ 547,844
Capitalization rate		—	—	—	—
Capitalized value		—	—	—	—
Discount factor	1.0	.8769	.8044	.7214	.6470
Discounted value	$7,875,000	$2,801,707	$2,553,753	$2,284,492	$ 354,455
Total					

Year 5	Year 6	Year 7	Year 8	Year 9	Year 10	Year 11
$ —	$ —	$ —	$ —	$ —	$ —	$ —
171,612	283,329	453,350	664,497	964,122	1,097,190	1,235,588
156,067	199,049	243,765	290,265	338,626	388,921	441,227
2,219,443	2,335,182	2,653,167	3,281,799	3,340,360	3,473,989	3,613,444
190,794	188,977	186,851	184,205	180,760	164,810	165,359
716,988	372,834	—	—	—	—	—
—	—	—	—	—	—	—
144,625	150,410	156,426	162,684	169,191	175,959	182,997
$3,599,529	$3,529,781	$3,693,559	$4,583,950	$4,993,069	$5,300,869	$ 5,638,615
(156,361)	(144,850)	(142,001)	(169,805)	(176,057)	(181,940)	(188,945)
$3,443,168	$3,384,931	$3,551,558	$4,414,145	$4,817,012	$5,118,929	$ 5,449,670
$1,891,341	$1,873,396	$1,948,332	$2,026,265	$2,107,314	$2,191,607	$ 2,279,273
46,794	48,666	50,613	52,638	54,743	56,933	59,210
467,943	486,661	506,128	526,373	547,428	569,325	592,098
614,176	638,743	664,792	690,863	718,499	747,239	777,128
100,000	100,000	100,000	100,000	100,000	100,000	100,000
$3,030,254	$3,147,465	$3,269,865	$3,396,139	$3,527,984	$3,665,104	$ 3,807,709
$ 412,914	$ 237,466	$ 281,693	$1,018,006	$1,289,028	$1,453,825	$ 1,641,961
—	—	—	—	—	—	.12
—	—	—	—	—	—	$13,683,006
.5803	.5204	.4667	.4186	.3754	.3367	.3367
$ 239,614	$ 123,577	$ 131,466	$ 426,137	$ 483,901	$ 489,503	$ 4,607,068
						$22,370,673

Endowment Resale Income. Forecasting endowment resale receipts requires an estimate of two key components: endowment fee appreciation rates, drawn from similar properties; and annual turnover, drawn from specific actuarial estimates for the subject and experience at similar properties. Endowment resale income is calculated below.

Period	Number of Turnover Units[1]	Average Resale Price[2]	Total Receipts	Amount Returned to Resident[3]	Amount Retained by Owner
Year 1	0	$105,000	$ 0	$ 0	$ 0
Year 2	2	$105,000	$ 210,000	$189,000	$ 21,000
Year 3	4	$105,000	$ 420,000	$378,000	$ 42,000
Year 4	6	$109,200	$ 655,200	$567,000	$ 88,200
Year 5	9	$113,568	$1,022,112	$850,000	$171,612

[1] Drawn from actuarial estimates in Table 10.8.
[2] Reflects 4% annual appreciation rate beginning in Year 4
[3] 90% of original purchase price

Reserve Fund Investment Income. Reserve fund investment income is the annual interest income earned on actual cash reserves set aside as required by state law to meet contractual obligations with residents.

Period	Reserve Fund	Investment Rate	Reserve Fund Interest Income
Year 1	$ 0	7%	$ 0
Year 2	$ 525,000	7%	$ 36,750
Year 3	$1,063,857	7%	$ 74,470
Year 4	$1,628,843	7%	$114,719
Year 5	$2,229,529	7%	$156,067

Great care should be exercised in estimating the level of cash reserves. Many states have complicated and confusing formulas for the cash reserve requirements.

Monthly Maintenance Fees. These fees are monthly charges to residents for a project's amenities, such as meals, housekeeping, recreation, and health care. As such, they are easily calculated as the number of residents multiplied by the applicable monthly charge per unit type. Second residents are commonly levied a surcharge monthly maintenance fee reflecting the additional expenditures necessary to provide amenities to these second occupants. Forecasting monthly maintenance fees is part of the feasibility analysis of the subject's anticipated endowment fees. In other words, these monthly fees must be determined from comparable facilities in the market. Also, monthly fees are set at levels to meet, at a minimum, the expenditures necessary to provide congregate living and health care to residents.

Nonmember Revenue. The subject has adopted a policy of allowing outside patients who have not paid the entry fee to be admitted to the health care beds provided on the subject campus when residents do not require them. These beds are offered to outside patients at rates determined by the market. An estimate of income from outside patients requires actuarial estimates of health care facility use by residents, since these patients have priority over outside patients. As the residents age and their health deteriorates, their use of the health care beds will grow until they fill all on-site health care beds. As a result, health care revenue from outside residents is typically high in the early years of a new CCRC and gradually declines to zero as fee-paying residents fill the health care beds. For illustration, residential care nonmember revenue is calculated below.

Period	Number of Residential Care Units	Member Use[1]	Nonmember Resident Use	Monthly Fee for Outside Residents/ Unit[2]	Annual Income
Year 1	20	2	18	$1,500	$324,000
Year 2	20	6	14	$1,560	$262,080
Year 3	20	11	9	$1,622	$175,219
Year 4	20	15	5	$1,689	$101,213
Year 5	20	20	0	$ 0	$ 0

[1] Per actual estimates in Table 10.8
[2] Assumes 4% annual increase

Comments

The subject's pro forma income stream demonstrates the complexity of estimating cash flows for a CCRC. In particular, the project's provision of a refundable endowment makes a computer analysis of cash flows necessary. Due to the limited direct competition within the subject's primary market area, the census of comparable projects was expanded beyond 25 miles. This was necessary to gauge market acceptance of the subject's proposed entry and maintenance fees by comparing them to similar projects in similar locations. To arrive at market rates for nonmember use of the residential care and skilled nursing facilities, separate market analyses were performed.

The forecast of cash flows from appreciated endowment fees required an estimation of two variables: resident turnover and annual appreciation rates. The resident turnover rate was drawn from actuarial estimates, shown in Table 10.8. Annual appreciation rates of 4% were estimated from local real estate trends and expectations of inflation. Facility C does not actuarially stabilize—that is, obtain a fixed resident turnover—until its tenth year, requiring a 10-year cash flow projection.

Our estimate of the appropriate discount rate reflects the development's three levels of on-site care. The rate blends the lower risk of the apartment units with the higher risk of the care units, which require specialized management. This case study illustrates the valuation of only one type of CCRC. Differences in endowment refundability, actuarial assumptions, reserve requirements, and fee-for-service programs make comparisons between CCRCs difficult.

Table 10.8. Case Study C, Actuarial Estimates

	Apartment Residents	Residential Care Residents	Skilled Nursing Residents	Total Residents	Unit Turnover
Year 0	97	—	—	97	—
Year 1	130	2	3	135	0
Year 2	162	6	5	173	2
Year 3	195	11	10	216	4
Year 4	193	15	16	224	6
Year 5	191	20	26	237	9
Year 6	189	20	38	247	12
Year 7	187	20	50	257	16
Year 8	185	20	50	255	20
Year 9	183	20	50	253	25
Year 10	180	20	50	250	25
Year 11	180	20	50	250	25

Case Study D

Project Description

Facility D is an existing 265-unit congregate rental and licensed residential care facility located in a densely populated, affluent, suburban location near a major metropolitan area on the West Coast. The project includes 220 congregate rental units and 45 residential care units with a total of 85 beds. This development was constructed in 1980 and was available for occupancy in March 1981. Full occupancy was achieved in the summer of 1983.

Facility D consists of four three-story, wood-frame improvements attached to a six-story, concrete-framed structure that contains the project's commons area and residential care units. Project residents receive two meals daily plus a continental breakfast, weekly housekeeping, and full indoor recreational activities. Personal living assistance is offered in the residential care units.

The facility is located in an area of mixed land uses and is bounded by other high-density residential structures, low-density residential development, and neighborhood commercial and retail development. The project's residents average 80 years of age, and the majority formerly resided within 10 miles of the subject site.

Table 10.9. Case Study D, Project and Valuation Statistics

Project Statistics	
Congregate rental units	220
Residential care units (beds)	45 (85)
Total units (occupancy)	265
Total rooms	487
Unit sizes—(sq. ft.)	
30—studios	420 avg.
154—1 bedrooms	560 avg.
36—2 bedrooms	820 avg.
45—residential care	445
Total building area (sq. ft.)	231,000
Building area/unit (sq. ft.)	871
Land area (sq. ft.)	216,600
Land area/unit (sq. ft.)	817
Valuation Statistics	
Land value/unit	$15,094
Improvement cost/unit[1]	$63,011
Improvement cost/sq. ft.[1]	$ 72.29
F F & E/unit[1]	$ 1,509
Monthly rentals—	
Studios	$1,025 ($2.44/unit)
1 bedroom	$1,350 ($2.41/unit)
2 bedroom	$1,800 ($2.20/unit)
Residential care rates—	
Private room—market	$ 1,500
Semi-private room—market	$ 825
SSI	$ 691
Average monthly rent—congregate	$ 1,328
Average monthly rent—residential care	$ 802
Vacancy allowance	5%
Miscellaneous income	0.9%
Double occupancy percentage	23.2%
Operating expense/unit	$ 8,455
Operating expense percentage	49.7%
Capitalization rate	11%
Total value/unit	$77,732
Total value/room	$42,298
Total value/sq. ft.	$ 89.17

[1] Replacement Cost New

Capitalization Process

The valuation of Facility D using the income capitalization approach requires the use of direct capitalization. This method applies an overall capitalization rate to a single-year, stabilized net operating income. This is appropriate where the income stream is equivalent to a stabilized fair market rate and operating expenses are stabilized at full occupancy.

A single-year pro forma stabilized income and expense cash flow estimate for Facility D is derived from a thorough analysis of the subject's historical cash flows. Two factors suggest that the subject's current rent structure represents market rates: market analysis of competitive facilities providing evidence that the subject rents are reasonable, and the subject's full or near-full occupancy at existing rents over the previous years. These factors suggest that current subject rents are neither too high nor too low and most likely represent market rates for the subject. An analysis of historical operating expenses shows minor fluctuations between years for individual expense items indicating no unusual one-time expense charges, and also a consistency of the subject's individual expenses with those of comparable projects. These factors indicate that the operating expenses have likely stabilized at full occupancy.

The pro forma estimate of revenues and expenses considers these historical operating results and market conditions at the time of the appraisal. It is necessary to forecast an annual pro forma income and expense for the subject for the year after the appraisal date, because an investor is more interested in cash flows in his or her first year of ownership than with historical cash flows. Historical and pro forma income and expense data are shown in Tables 10.10 and 10.11.

Table 10.10. Case Study D, Operating History

	1985		1986	
	%	% EGI	%	% EGI
Average occupancy—congregate	94.6%		95.9%	
Average occupancy—resident care	97.3%		92.1%	
Average rental—congregate	$ 1,273		$ 1,334	
Average rental—residential care	$ 746		$ 769	
Gross income				
Congregate rental units—				
30—studios	$ 348,192		$ 353,662	
154—1 bedrooms	2,321,365		2,460,003	
36—2 bedrooms	690,923		707,200	
Total	$3,360,480	77.4%	$3,520,865	77.8%
Residential care beds—				
Private beds—market	$ 87,100		$ 84,777	
Semi-private beds—market	373,968		381,009	
SSI beds	300,048		318,255	
Total	$ 761,116	17.5%	$ 784,041	17.3%
Double occupancy changes	$ 176,400	4.1%	$ 178,050	3.9%
Miscellaneous income	$ 46,289	1.0%	$ 39,993	0.9%
Total income	$4,344,285	100.0%	$4,522,949	100.0%
Expenses				
Real estate taxes	$ 201,580	4.6%	$ 205,612	4.6%
Insurance	75,000	1.7	102,500	2.3
Management	195,493	4.5	203,532	4.5
G & A	177,289	4.1	196,592	4.4
Activities	40,000	0.9	42,103	0.9
Marketing	20,000	0.5	19,205	0.4
Utilities	226,983	5.2	269,072	6.0
Maintenance	99,100	2.3	126,997	2.8
Transportation	36,212	0.8	38,173	0.8
Housekeeping	186,003	4.3	202,266	4.5
Dietary	592,666	13.6	627,888	13.9
Residential care	129,167	3.0	148,700	3.3
Total expenses	$1,979,493	45.6%	$2,182,640	48.3%
Net income	$2,364,792	54.4%	$2,340,309	51.7%

Table 10.11. Case Study D, Pro Forma Income and Expenses

	Pro Forma $	% EGI
Average occupancy—congregate	95%	
Average occupancy—residential care	95%	
Average rental—congregate	$ 1,328	
Average rental—residential care	$ 802	
Potential gross income—		
Congregate rental units—		
34—studios @ $1,025/mo.	$ 48,200	
154—1 bedrooms @ $1,350/mo.	2,494,800	
36—2 bedrooms @ $1,800/mo.	777,600	
Total	$ 3,690,600	81.9
Residential care units—		
5—private beds—market	$ 90,000	
40—Semi-private beds—market	396,000	
40—SSI beds	371,680	
Total	$ 817,680	18.1
Double occupancy charges	$ 183,600	4.1
Miscellaneous income	$ 40,000	0.9
Gross income	$ 4,731,880	105.0
Less: vacancy & collection losses	$ (225,414)	5.0
Effective gross income	$ 4,506,466	100.0
Expenses		
Operating expenses	$ 2,140,571	47.5
Replacement reserves	100,000	2.2
Total	$ 2,240,571	49.7
Net income	$ 2,265,895	50.3
Capitalization rate	11%	
Capitalized value	$20,599,045	

Capitalization Rate

A capitalization rate for the subject's pro forma stabilized net operating income is drawn from two methods:

1. A comparison of the subject to indicated overall capitalization rates derived from sales of comparable properties
2. A weighted average band-of-investment technique

Deriving capitalization rates for the subject from comparable sales is complicated because the subject contains two very different types of housing: independent congregate living and residential care. Sales of comparable properties provided the following capitalization rate ranges.

Congregate facilities	9.5%–11.0%
Residential care facilities	10.0%–12.5%

Compared with the above sales, the subject is an average or typical facility with regard to rent structure, competitive environment, location, amenities, and overall quality. This would suggest a capitalization rate in the middle of the indicated ranges. The large number of independent living units provides evidence for a slightly larger capitalization rate. The overall capitalization rate for the subject derived from market sales is calculated as

Revenue Source	Percent of Revenue		Comparable OAR		Weighted OAR
Congregate	80%	×	10.5%	=	8.4%
Residential care	20%	×	11.0%	=	2.2%
Calculated OAR for subject					10.6%

To supplement the above analysis, a band-of-investment technique was used, based on the following assumptions:

Mortgage loan-to-value ratio	75%
Equity loan-to-value ratio	25%
Mortgage loan market terms	10%, 30 years
Equity dividend rate	12%–15%

These assumptions were drawn from discussions with lenders and developers active in the retirement housing industry. A band-of-investment calculation using the above assumptions yields a higher overall capitalization rate.

Component	Loan-to-Value Ratio		Annual Rate		Weighted Average
Mortgage	0.75	×	.105	=	.079
Equity	0.25	×	.135	=	.034
Weighted average OAR					11.3%

Using these two methods, an appropriate overall capitalization rate of 11% for the subject is derived. This conclusion considered several factors, including the subject's growingly competitive environment, large number of units, and competitive position.

Comments

This highly successful facility benefits by its location in an affluent suburban location. High rents and land and improvement costs reflect the neighborhood's high cost of living. As shown in the subject's operating history, operating revenues and expenses stabilized shortly after full occupancy was achieved in 1984.

The subject is located in an actively competitive elderly housing market. However, the area has a large population base of 500,000 people within a 10-mile radius of the site creating demand for elderly housing. Existing rents were consistent with market rates. The development has a waiting list of six to 12 months, ensuring full occupancy in the short run. Historical operating expense ratios were consistent with comparable projects. The subject's expenses incorporate the additional costs required to provide personal living assistance to a large percentage of the project's residents. The capitalization rate derived for the subject's stabilized income stream reflects an actively competitive market, high rental rates, the large number of subject units, and the specialized management necessary for a combination-care project such as the subject.

Glossary

Definitions marked by an asterisk are taken from *The Dictionary of Real Estate Appraisal* (Chicago: American Institute of Real Estate Appraisers, 1984).

AAHA—The American Association of Homes for the Aging, a national organization representing operators and owners of nonprofit homes for the elderly and related services. AAHA homes are sponsored by religious, fraternal, labor, private, and government organizations.

AARP—The American Association of Retired People, the United States' largest association for the elderly.

Absorption rate—The rate at which properties for sale or lease can be successfully marketed in a given area; usually used in forecasting sales or leasing activity.*

Accommodation fee—See "Entrance fee."

Amenities package—See "Services."

Assisted living—See "Residential care facility."

Board and care—See "Residential care facility."

Condominium—A form of fee-simple ownership giving the owner full and transferable title only to the living unit, rather than the lot and all improvements. Common areas such as sidewalks, stairways, hallways, and recreation facilities are usually owned jointly with other residents.

Congregate housing—Multiunit, usually rental, housing for the elderly that is characterized by an array of services designed to aid a resident's independence. Common services include housekeeping, transportation, organized activities, security, and grounds maintenance. Although most units have kitchens, congregate facilities usually serve at least one meal a day in a central dining area to ease a resident's workload and encourage socialization. Most congregate facilities do not provide health care; they are targeted to the fully ambulatory and healthy. Residents are usually between 75 and 85 years old, and tend to be female and widowed.

Continuing care contract—A legally binding agreement between a resident and a CCRC or lifecare facility, delineating what shelter and services will be provided to the resident over a specified time, and what obligations—including lump-sum or monthly payments—are required of the resident. These contracts are essentially an insurance agreement: in return for the resident's entrance fee, housing and care are provided for life. The contracts are also known as lifecare contracts, entrance fee agreements, sustaining gift contracts, occupancy agreements, accommodation fee agreements, member trust fund contracts, founders' fee contracts, community residence agreements, and residence and care agreements.

Continuing-care retirement center (CCRC)—A newer, modified version of the lifecare center that is distinguished by its method of financing, which emphasizes either a monthly maintenance fee and a partially or fully refundable entrance fee, or services on a fee-for-service basis. CCRCs are licensed in many states. Like the lifecare center, the CCRC includes a residential complex, with possible units ranging from cottages to high-rise apartments; a commons area including administrative, dining, and activities areas; and the health center, usually composed of nursing beds and an infirmary or clinic. The growth of CCRCs was a response to financial troubles in the lifecare industry that surfaced in the 1970s. See also "Life-care center."

Continuum of care—A spectrum of services and facilities offered by a housing project as a way to meet the needs of seniors of varying independent living capabilities. The continuum of care idea is designed so that the elderly do not have to move from facility to facility if their physical or mental condition changes.

Cooperative—A form of leasehold interest ownership in which residents hold shares in a corporation having ownership of the entire project. Ownership of cooperative shares allows a resident to occupy a housing unit exclusively into perpetuity. Shareholder residents usually pay a monthly fee to the cooperative covering operating and maintenance costs.

Elderly—In general, all those persons 65 years of age and older. Further delineated by the "young-old" (65 to 75 years), "old" (75 to 85 years), and "old-old" (85 years and up).

Empty nester—A pre-retiree, generally over 55 years old, who is looking to move from a large, single-family, detached home to a smaller home, condominium, or townhouse. Many empty nesters are married couples with no dependents.

Endowment, endowment fee—See "Entrance fee."

Entrance fee—A one-time fee paid by a resident to a CCRC or lifecare facility. Fees range from $5,000 to more than $1,000,000, and can be refundable, partially refundable, or nonrefundable. Entrance fees can be marketed as prepaid housing and health care. The fee is used as a method of privately financing the development of the facility, usually combined with other forms of financing. Entrance fees are also known as endowment fees, buy-in fees, accommodation fees, founders' fees, membership fees, or admission fees.

Fee for service—A method of offering project services individually, with residents paying for only those services actually used.

Financial feasibility study—1) An analysis that determines whether a project will fulfill the economic requirements of the investor. 2) An analysis of the profitability of a specific real estate undertaking in terms of the criteria of a specific market or investor.*

Income capitalization approach—A set of procedures in which an appraiser derives a value indication for income-producing property by converting anticipated benefits into property value. This conversion is accomplished either by 1) capitalizing a single year's income expectancy or annual average of several years' income expectancies at a market-derived capitalization rate or a capitalization rate that reflects a specified income pattern, return on investment, and change in the value of the investment; or 2) discounting the annual cash flows for the holding period and the reversion at a specified yield rate.*

Independent housing—Housing that allows the resident to live in a totally independent manner and does not provide care or services designed for those with physical or mental limitations. Units include houses, cottages, townhouses, condominiums, apartments, or retirement residences. Congregate facilities, as defined above, are not included in this category.

Intermediate care facility (ICF)—A licensed facility which stands between residential care and skilled care in the level of health care provided. It is aimed at persons not capable of fully independent living who need non-continuous medical, nursing, and rehabilitative services in addition to room and board.

Lifecare—A campus-type elderly project offering a continuum of care: independent living coupled with intermediate or skilled nursing care. Lifecare centers offer the same services as congregate centers—housekeeping, meals, transportation, security—with the addition of living assistance and medical care. Traditional lifecare facilities require an endowment fee that guarantees the resident lifetime residence and medical care, as well as a monthly maintenance fee. Because of several bankruptcies in this industry in the 1970s, many facilities have curtailed guaranteed services in favor of a fee-for-service approach. See also "Continuing-care retirement center."

Maintenance fee—A monthly service fee which can cover a variety of costs incurred in a senior facility, including meals, utilities, housekeeping, medical care, maintenance, and security, without creating excess income. Usually associated with buy-in projects such as CCRCs.

Market area—A geographic area or political jurisdiction in which alternative, similar properties effectively compete with the subject property in the minds of probable, potential purchasers and users.*

Market rent—The rental income that a property would most probably command in the open market; indicated by current rents paid and asked for comparable space as of the date of the appraisal.*

Market share—The portion of a trade area's potential, e.g., retail sales to be generated, office space to be absorbed, that can be attributed to a proposed facility; based on known market strength and the property's position relative to comparable, competitive facilities.* It is measured through market saturation analysis.

Market study—The process of determining the general market conditions affecting the property to be marketed, including historical and potential levels of supply and demand; as distinguished from marketability, which determines a property's capacity to be absorbed, sold, or leased.*

Medicaid—A medical financial assistance program administered by all states (except Arizona) offering benefits to the poor, disabled, and elderly. Medicaid can reimburse SNFs and ICFs for the long-term care of qualifying seniors.

Medicare—A nationwide medical insurance program administered by the Social Security Administration for people 65 and over and certain disabled people, available without regard to income. Medicare can reimburse skilled nursing facilities for the first 20 days of patient medical care.

Monthly service fee—See "Maintenance fee."

NAILC—The National Association of Independent Living Centers, a trade group established to promote professionalism and excellence in the development and operation of housing for the independent elderly.

NASLI—The National Association of Senior Living Industries, a resource network for organizations, professionals, and private citizens in the elderly housing field.

NCOA—The National Council on Aging, a national, nonprofit membership organization that serves as a resource for development, publications, special programs, and training to meet older people's needs.

Nursing home—See "Skilled nursing facility."

Personal care—See "Residential care facility."

Primary market research—Use of surveys, questionnaires, or focus study groups to measure potential interest or demand for a specific proposed elderly development. Distinguished from secondary market research which measures demand using macrodemographic data extracted from the U.S. census.

Residential care facility (RCF)—A facility, commonly known as a board and care facility, offering more care than a congregate center but less than an ICF or SNF. The resident receives daily assistance with meals, dressing, personal hygiene, transportation, housekeeping, and mobility as necessary, in a private or shared room. Facilities are licensed and may offer limited health care.

Retirement community—A large, privately-built development which focuses on young retirees by emphasizing outdoor recreational amenities, such as golf courses, swimming pools, tennis courts, and club complexes. Housing options offered are usually for purchase and include single-family homes, duplexes, townhouses, and condominium units. Also called a retirement resort or retirement new town. This type of senior development now houses about 30% of retirees. Examples include Rossmoor Leisure World in Laguna Hills, California, and Sun City, Arizona.

Retirement villages and subdivisions—Large, planned retirement developments. Retirement villages usually hold from 1,000 to 5,000 people, while subdivisions average 500 residents. The variety in this category of housing is enormous, ranging from single-family homes and low- and high-rise apartments to mobile home parks. Villages often offer recreational activities and security, while subdivisions depend more on the surrounding community and offer amenities that may be limited to a multipurpose room. Examples are Orange Gardens in Kissimmee, Florida and Leisure Village West, Manchester Township, New Jersey.

Saturation ratio—The rate quantifying the saturation of one elderly housing project within a defined market area. Calculated as the number of elderly housing units in any one project divided by the total number of income- and age-qualifying seniors within a market area.

Service fee—See "Maintenance fee."

Services—The amenities available to residents of an elderly housing development. The newest forms of senior housing, such as CCRCs and congregate housing, are defined by their extensive services or amenities package. Common services available at these projects include food and dietary service, transportation, housekeeping and maintenance, laundry service, security, recreation facilities and services, adult day care, and various medical services ranging from a pharmacy to a clinic or skilled nursing care.

Skilled nursing facility (SNF)—A state-licensed facility commonly known as a nursing home, which provides around-the-clock nursing care for convalescent patients. This form of care, one level below acute hospital care, includes restorative, physical, occupational, and other therapy.

Supplemental security income (SSI)—A state-regulated, federally financed financial assistance program for the elderly residing in residential care facilities. SSI benefits are paid directly to an individual who in turn pays for services provided by the RCF.

Selected Bibliography

Books

American Institute of Real Estate Appraisers. *The Appraisal of Real Estate*, 9th ed. Chicago, 1987.

Carstens, Diane Y. *Site Planning and Design for the Elderly*. New York: Van Nostrand Reinhold, 1985.

Chellis, Robert D., James F. Seagle, Jr., and Barbara Mackey Seagle. *Congregate Housing for Older People*. Lexington, Mass.: Lexington Books, 1985.

Gold, Margaret. *Guide to Housing Alternatives for Older Citizens*. Mount Vernon, N.Y.: Consumers Union, 1985.

Hancock, Judith Ann, ed. *Housing the Elderly*. Piscataway, N.J.: Center for Urban Policy Research, Rutgers University, 1987.

National Association for Senior Living Industries. *The Directory of Senior Living Industries*. Annapolis, Md., 1986.

Parker, Rosetta E. *Housing for the Elderly: The Handbook for Managers*. Chicago: Institute of Real Estate Management, 1984.

Pifer, Alan, and Lydia Bronte. *Our Aging Society*. New York: W.W. Norton, 1986.

Raper, A. T. *National Continuing Care Directory*. Glenview, Ill.: Scott, Foresman & Co., published for the American Association of Retired Persons, 1984 (AARP Books, 400 S. Edward Street, Mount Prospect, IL 60056).

U.S. Senate. Special Committee on Aging. *Aging America: Trends and Projections*. 1985-86 edition. Prepared in conjunction with the American Association of Retired Persons, the Federal Council on the Aging, and the Administration on Aging. Washington, D.C.: U.S. Department of Health and Human Services, 1985.

Winklevoss, Howard E., and Alwyn V. Powell. *Continuing Care Retirement Communities: An Empirical, Financial and Legal Analysis*. Homewood, Ill.: Richard D. Irwin, for Pension Research Council, Wharton School, University of Pennsylvania, 1984.

Worley, H. Wilson. *Retirement Living Alternatives USA—The Inside Story*. Clemson, S.C.: Columbia House, 1982.

Periodicals

Adams, Eli. "The Graying of America: New Builder Opportunity in a Growing Demographic Market." *Professional Builder*, August 1984, pp. 135-151.

Adams, Eli, ed. "The Graying of America." *Professional Builder*, September 1985, pp. 66-83.

_____. "The Graying of America." *Professional Builder*, April 1986, pp. 68-83.

_____. "Havens for Retirees and Empty Nesters." *Professional Builder*, February 1983, pp. 104-110.

Anderson, Fonda. "Retirement Center Answered Senior Needs." *Tampa Bay Business,* February 9-15, 1986, p. 1.

Baum, Allyn Z. "Would a Life-Care Community Be Right for You?" *Medical Economics,* March 7, 1983, pp. 132-136.

Becker, Helmut A. "CCRC Development Needs Team Approach." *Contemporary Long-Term Care,* February 1986, pp. 52-64.

Beckerman, David S. "Bright Prospects for Rental Retirement Housing." *Urban Land,* November 1986, pp. 6-9.

Birenbaum, A. "Aging and Housing: A Note on How Housing Expresses Social Status." *Journal of Housing for the Elderly,* vol. 2, no. 1 (1984), pp. 33-40.

Birkner, Edward C. "Adult Community With All the Extras." *Professional Builder,* September 1984, p. 66.

Brecht, Susan B. "Lifecare Comes of Age." *Urban Land,* August 1984, pp. 14-17.

Bresnick, Peggy S. "5 Levels of Congregate Care Succeed for Elderly Rentals." *Multi-Housing News,* October 1984, pp. 1, 52.

——————. "Extensive Rec, Open Unit Design Suit Active Retirement Market." *Multi-Housing News,* March 1984, pp. 16, 21.

——————. "Projects Suited to 50-Plus Market Range from Subsidized to Luxury." *Multi-Housing News,* March 1984, pp. 1, 16.

Buffington, A. D. "Three Approaches to Residential Care." *Provider,* April 1986, pp. 20-22.

"Building Types Study 610: Housing for the Elderly—Sheltered Independence: Life After 65." *Architectural Record,* February 1985, pp. 95-113.

Butler, N. G. "Optimal Long-Term Health Care for the Elderly: An Acute Care Hospital's Perspective." *Topics in Health Care Financing,* Fall 1984, pp. 57-65.

Carpenter, Kimberly, and Irene Pave. "What's Putting New Life into 'Life Care' Communities." *Business Week,* March 3, 1986, pp. 108-110.

Cole, Richard A. "More Sophisticated Financings Help Life Care Centers Avert Failure." *Modern Healthcare,* February 1983, pp. 129-131.

Cole, Richard A., and John A. Marr. "Life Care Retirement Centers: The Importance of the Entry Fee Fund." *Healthcare Financial Management,* July 1984, pp. 84-90.

Corpuz, Chris, and Judith Holloway. "Meeting the Elderly's Demand for Housing." *Liberty Street Chronicle,* August 1985, pp. 26-27.

Covaleski, John. "5 Invest $100 Million in Housing for Elderly." *Pensions & Investment Age,* December 8, 1986, pp. 37-38.

Curran, Stroud, and Susan Brecht. "A Perspective on Risks for Lifecare Projects." *Real Estate Finance Journal,* Summer 1985, pp. 64-69.

Dentzer, Susan. "Has Sun City Come of Age?" *Newsweek,* May 6, 1985, pp. 68-70.

Elliott, Laura. "What About Mom and Dad?" *The Washingtonian,* March 1985, pp. 104-124.

Eramian, Bob. "Staging a Successful Turnaround." *Contemporary Long-Term Care*, February 1986, pp. 48-55.

Faircloth, H. Spencer. "Skeptical Lenders Demand Details for Retirement Projects." *Multi-Housing News*, June 1985, pp. 32-33.

Federal Research Press. *Retirement Housing Report.* Monthly.

Fisher, Anne B. "The New Game in Health Care: Who Will Profit?" *Fortune*, March 4, 1985, pp. 138-143.

Graaskamp, James A. "Identification and Delineation of Real Estate Market Research." *Real Estate Issues*, Spring/Summer 1985, pp. 6-12.

Graham, Judith. "Demand Should Foster Growth in Retirement Center Industry." *Modern Healthcare*, April 24, 1987, pp. 52-58.

"Growing Opportunities Seen in Senior Citizen Housing." *Real Estate Outlook*, Summer 1986, pp. 1-2, 30-31.

Grubb & Ellis. "Housing for the Elderly." *Investor Outlook*, Second Quarter 1986.

Henderson, Michael J. "Lifestyles for the Elderly: Best of Both Worlds (Congregate Living Facility)." *Mortgage Banking*, December 1985, pp. 27, 32-39.

Horn, Dennis M. "Developing and Financing Retirement Center Housing." *Real Estate Finance*, Summer 1985, pp. 26-37.

Horowitz, Judith, and J. Bruce Ryan. "Structuring the Life-Care Contract to Minimize Financial Risk." *Topics in Health Care Financing*, Fall 1984, pp. 66-76.

Hunt, Michael E., Allan G. Feldt, Robert W. Marans, Leon A. Pastalan, and Kathleen L. Vakalo. "Retirement Communities: An American Original." *Journal of Housing for the Elderly*, Winter 1983, pp. 1-278.

Jeck, Allister M., and June E. Carlson. "Retirement Housing: Exploring the Gray Area of Housing's Gray Market." *Real Estate Finance*, Winter 1986, pp. 57-68.

Kaufmann, Gadi. "Selling to Seniors: It's a Lively Market." *Real Estate Today*, June 1985, pp. 11-13.

Kelder, James, ed. *Housing the Elderly.* April 1985, May 1987, and June 1987. Silver Springs: CD Publications.

Koff, Theodore H. "Developing Successful Housing for the Elderly." *Real Estate Review*, Summer 1986, pp. 90-92.

Laing, Susan, and Linda F. Little. "The Management of Federally Subsidized Housing for Elderly Residents." *Journal of Property Management*, November/December 1985, pp. 9-12.

Lane, L. F. "Understanding Long Term Care Policy and the Consequences for Reimbursement (New Dollars for Long Term Care: Proceedings from the PRIDE Institute Conference, December 1982)." *Journal of Long Term Home Health Care*, vol. 2, no. 2 (1983), pp. 7-15.

"Location, Rec, Food Service Point to Profitable Congregate." *Multi-Housing News*, March 1985, pp. 29-30.

McMullin, DeWayne. "Common Financial Problems Encountered by CCRCs." *Contemporary Long-Term Care*, February 1986, pp. 50-51.

Markov, Nancy. " 'Live Rent Free' Marketing Sells Empty Nesters on Rentals —Glenview, Ill." *Multi-Housing News*, December 1985, p. 20.

_____. "Upstairs Visitor's Quarters Appeal to Rich Empty Nesters." *Multi-Housing News*, April 1985, pp. 8-9.

Matchison, S., and M. H. Leeds. "Housing Policy for Older Americans in the 1980s: An Overview." *Journal of Housing for the Elderly*, Spring/Summer 1983, pp. 7-13.

"The Mature Market—An Age of Promise." *Real Estate Quarterly*, Fall 1985, pp. 3-5.

Mitchell, John, ed. "McKendree's Winning Combination: Quality Care and Low Cost." *Contemporary Long-Term Care*, November 1985, pp. 35-36, 62.

Mitchell, John, ed. *Contemporary Long Term Care*, Vol. 10, No. 6 (June 1987). Nashville, Tenn.: Advantage Publishing.

National Association of Independent Living Centers. *Journal of Independent Living*, Spring 1987, Summer 1987, and Fall 1987.

National Council on Aging. *Senior Housing News*. First, Second, and Third Quarter, 1987.

Newman, Sandra J. "Housing Policy for the Elderly: The Shape of Things to Come." *Generations*, Spring/Summer 1985, pp. 14-17.

Nutt, William. "147-Unit Retirement Complex Offers Health, Living Facilities." *Multi-Housing News*, January 1985, pp. 22, 27.

_____. "Lifecare Resort Community Preserves Residents' Capital— Chapel Hill, N.C." *Multi-Housing News*, February 1985, p. 16.

"Older Americans to Provide Growing Multifamily Market." *Nation's Building News*, April 15, 1985, p. 7.

Otten, Alan L. "U.S. Agencies Awaken to the Need for More Data on Nation's Elderly." *The Wall Street Journal*, December 9, 1986, p. 36.

Parker, Rosetta E. "The Future of Elderly Housing." *Journal of Property Management*, May/June 1984, pp. 12-16.

Parmiter, Don. "Developing for the Over-50s Market." *Urban Land*, February 1984, pp. 2-7.

Pastalan, Leon A. "Demographic Characteristics." *Journal of Housing for the Elderly*, Spring/Summer 1983, pp. 85-86.

_____. "Retirement Communities." *Generations*, Spring/Summer 1985, pp. 26-30.

Pynoos, J. "Option for Mid-Upper-Income Elders: Continuum of Care Retirement Communities." *Generations*, Fall 1985, pp. 31-33.

Rasmussen, John A. "Retirement Community Development: New Trends in Marketing and Financing Concepts." *Real Estate Issues*, Fall/Winter 1986, pp. 19-26.

"Retirement Housing—A Maturing Market." *Builder*, June 1985, pp. 71-91.

"Retirement Housing Experts Debate Selling vs. Renting." *Multi-Housing News*, April 1986, p. 19.

Riche, Martha Farnsworth. "Retirement's Lifestyle Pioneers." *American Demographics*, January 1986, pp. 42-44, 50, 52-54, 56.

Ricks, Thomas E. "People's Perception of the Elderly as Being Poor Is Starting to Fade." *The Wall Street Journal*, December 19, 1985, p. 31.

Rogers, Steve. "Retirement Life Planners Building Success in Retirement Housing." *Contemporary Long-Term Care*, May 1986, pp. 60-63.

Rohrer, Robert L., and Robert Bibb. "Marketing: The CCRC Challenge." *Contemporary Long-Term Care*, May 1986, pp. 41-58.

Rose, Aaron M. "Continuing Care Retirement Centers: An Expansion Opportunity." *American Health Care Association Journal*, May 1983, pp. 36-39.

_____. "Entrepreneurs Reshaping Lifecare." *Modern Healthcare*, July 1984, pp. 148-153.

Seiler, Stephen R. "How to Develop Retirement Communities for Profit." *Real Estate Review*, Fall 1986, pp. 70-75.

Senior Citizens Marketing Group. *Mature Market Report*. Dallas, Tex.: Allyn Kramer, vol. 1, no. 2.

"Senior Housing Demands Mature Attitude by Developers." *Multi-Housing News*, July 1985, p. 84.

"Seniors Aging in Place Spur Debate on Health Care." *Multi-Housing News*, March 1986, pp. 25-26.

"Seniors Reduce Space Needs, Accept High Densities." *Multi-Housing News*, July 1986, pp. 21-24.

Seip, David E. "Doing It Over Again." *Contemporary Long Term Care*, May 1987, pp. 28-29.

Shashaty, Andre. "Competition Increases in Retirement Housing." *Multi-Housing News*, March 1985, pp. 62, 64.

_____. "Congregate Condos Offer Elderly Ownership, Flexibility." *Multi-Housing News*, April 1985, pp. 16-17.

_____. "Studies Show That Tax Reform Will Kill Rental Housing." *Multi-Housing News*, March 1985, pp. 9-11.

Sims, William B. "Financing Strategies for Long-Term Care Facilities." *Healthcare Financial Management*, March 1984, pp. 42-54.

Smart, Eric. "With a Maturing Population, Age Is Only Part of the Picture." *Urban Land*, May 1983, pp. 32-33.

Stockman, Leslie Ensor. "Hotel Giant Throws Hat into Life Care Market." *Builder*, October 1985, p. 70.

Thornton, James. "A New Wrinkle in Cooperatives." *Corporate Report Minnesota*, October 1986, pp. 96-103.

Topolnicki, Denise M. "The Broken Promise of Life-Care Communities." *Money*, April 1985, pp. 150-157.

Townsend, Bickley. "Eating Our Seed Corn." *American Demographics*, January 1986, pp. 46-48.

Valiante, John. "The Capital Requirements for Long-Term Care Services." *Healthcare Financial Management*, April 1984, pp. 84-90.

Vescovi, Jim. "2nd Tier City Demand Could Spark Good Year." *Multi-Housing News*, March 1985, pp. 56-57.

Ward, Matthews E. "Congregate Living Arrangements: The Financing Option." *Topics in Health Care Financing*, Fall 1984, pp. 34-45.

Weeden, Joel. "The Housing Compendium." *Generations*, Spring/Summer 1985, pp. 9-10.

Williams, Thomas P., MAI, and John A. Rasmussen. "Feasibility and Valuation of a Continuing Care Retirement Community." *The Appraisal Journal*, July 1985, pp. 354-370.

"What It Takes to Make a Go of Retirement Housing." *Professional Builder/Apartment Business*, June 1985, p. 24.

Worley, H. Wilson. "Housing Alternatives for Retirees." *Real Estate Today*, October 1983, pp. 22-24.

Zeisel, John. "Apartments Offer Alternative for Seniors." *Nation's Building News*, April 15, 1985, p. 6.

_____. "How to Design, Market and Operate Housing for Seniors." *Nation's Building News*, March 25, 1985, pp. 6-7.

Zinsser, John. "Housing: Your Exciting New Options." *50 Plus*, March 1985, pp. 28-60.

Reports, Monographs, and Conference Papers

American Association of Homes for the Aging. *Obtaining Capital for Housing and Services for the Elderly*. Washington, D.C.: AAHA and Real Estate Financial Services, 1984.

_____. *Market and Economic Feasibility Studies: Guidelines for Continuing Care Retirement Communities*. Washington, D.C., 1984.

American Association of Retired Persons. *Housing Options for Older Americans*. Washington, D.C., 1984.

American Health Care Association. *Trends and Strategies in Long Term Care*. Washington, D.C., 1985.

Citizens for Better Nursing Home Care in Santa Barbara County [Calif.]. *Consumer's Directory of Long-Term Care Facilities and Alternative Services*, 1984-85 ed.

Cloud, Deborah A., ed. *Continuing Care: Issues for Nonprofit Providers*. Washington, D.C.: American Association of Homes for the Aging, 1985.

Donahue, Wilma T., Maire McGuire Thompson, and D. J. Curren, eds. *Congregate Housing for Older People—An Urgent Need, A Growing Demand*. International Center for Social Gerontology, selected conference papers, November 11-12, 1975. Washington, D.C., 1975.

Coopers & Lybrand. *A Layman's Guide to Health Care V: Continuing Care Retirement Communities*. New York, 1985.

Cosby, Robert L., Jr., and Teri Flynn. *Housing for Older Adults: Options and Answers*. Washington, D.C.: National Council on the Aging, 1986.

Federal National Mortgage Association. *Forum III: Housing for the Retired*. Washington, D.C., 1979.

Laventhol & Horwath. *Life Care Retirement Center Industry*. Philadelphia, 1985.

_____. *The Senior Living Industry*. Philadelphia, 1986.

_____. *The Nursing Home Industry, 1986: A Capsule View*. Philadelphia, 1986.

MacKelvie, Charles F. "Life Care Contracts: A Developer's, Lender's and Manager's Perspective." Paper presented at the National Health Lawyers Association Conference on Long-Term Care and The Law, San Diego, February 5-7, 1986.

Moore, Jim. *Retirement Housing Market Feasibility*. Fort Worth: Moore Diversified Services, 1986.

Murata Outland Associates. *Understanding Elderly Housing*. Denver, 1985.

National Association of Senior Living Industries. *NASLI Conference in Review*. Annapolis, Md., 1987.

Pynoos, J., V. Regnier, and T. K. O'Brien. *Continuum of Care Retirement Community Project—Final Report*. Los Angeles: Institute for Policy and Program Development, Andrus Gerontology Center, University of Southern California, 1984.

Real Estate Research Corporation. *Rental Retirement Housing: New Opportunities*. Chicago, 1985.

Rohrer, Robert L., and Robert Bibb. *Product Segmentation and Marketing Challenges in the Senior Housing Industry*. Technical Bulletin M-1. Annapolis, Md.: National Association of Senior Living Industries, April 1986.

Turner, Lloyd, and Eglute Mangum. *Report on the Housing Choices of Older Americans*. Bryn Mawr, Pa.: Graduate School of Social Work and Social Research, Bryn Mawr College, 1982.

U.S. Department of Health and Human Services. Administration on Aging. *A Profile of Older Americans*. Washington, D.C.: American Association of Retired Persons, 1984.

U.S. Library of Congress. Congressional Research Service. *Life Care Communities: Description and Current Issues*. Washington, D.C.: U.S. Government Printing Office, December 23, 1985.

Weeden, Joel, and Robert Newcomer. *Redefining Life Care: Trends in Development, Regulation and Financing*. San Francisco: Aging Health Policy Center, University of California at San Francisco, 1985.

Associations and Groups for the Elderly

American Association of Homes for the Aging (AAHA)
1050 17th St., N.W.
Washington, D.C. 20036
(202) 296-5960

Represents operators and owners of nonprofit homes for the elderly and related services. AAHA has produced several publications on continuing care and other subjects.

American Association of Retired People
1909 K St., N.W.
Washington, D.C. 20049
(202) 872-4700

Largest association for the elderly in the United States. Lobbies for senior-related legislation and provides information, insurance, travel programs, educational programs, and other services to its members.

National Association of Independent Living Centers
1501 Lee Highway, Suite 205
Arlington, VA 22209
(703) 243-9100

Established to promote professionalism and excellence among developers, operators, and consultants of housing for the independent elderly.

National Association of Senior Living Industries
125 Cathedral St.
Annapolis, MD 21401
(301) 263-0991

A resource network for organizations, professionals, and private citizens in the elderly housing field.

National Council on Aging
600 Maryland Ave., N.W.
Washington, D.C.
(202) 479-1200

A national, nonprofit membership organization that serves as a resource for development, publications, special programs, and training to meet older people's needs.